SHATTER THE BOX

A guide to revolutionizing
Christian education

Stefanee Tolbert

Table of Contents

Acknowledgements

A special thank you to my husband, Trent, who has been there every step of the way. He encourages me and speaks truth into my life (even when I 'm difficult and don't want to hear it). He says I am like a kite, flying as high as I can go. He is the one holding that string keeping me grounded and from crashing into a tree. I am so grateful.

Thank you to my four amazing kiddos. I started this thing hoping to create a space for you to learn and grow both academically and spiritually, and you are the driving force behind everything I do. I am so proud to be your mommy.

I'd also like to thank my momma! She is my partner in crime, and I would never want to build this dream without her. We are polar opposites and I need her more than she will ever truly realize. She is the secret to my success.

Thank you could never suffice for the unbelievable team I have. I love each of them so much and truly wish I could show them how much they each add to the environment of the academy.

Thank you to my family. My parents, sisters, brothers, nieces, and nephews. There is no one who could ever convince me that a better family exists, and I am so grateful for your love and support. Knowing that you are loved unconditionally is such a rare gift, and I have that in my family.

To everyone who has believed the best in me throughout my life, I want to say thank you. Your love and support has not gone unnoticed and I am so grateful.

Most of all I am grateful for Jesus, the original box shatterer. Everything I am, and all I will ever be is because of Him.

Connect with

STEFANEE

Stolbert@lcasulphur.com

Facebook: stefaneetolbert

Instagram: stefaneetolbert

Why This Book

This book comes from a place of strong belief in private Christian schools. The truth is that for far too long, our society has told us all the things we are not and has viewed far too many Christian schools as a joke. This book is intended to challenge this idea. My heart wants to see Christian schools rise up. I hope to encourage you to challenge the status quo, to not only think outside the box—to shatter the box. I long to see excellence rise up within us. It isn't about how many students are in your school, it's about the quality of education you are truly providing.

I am the co-founder, visionary, and principal of Life Christian Academy (LCA) in Sulphur, Louisiana. I am running on a mission to encourage, equip, and empower Christian educators to provide the very best education possible. In living out this mission, I have the incredible opportunity to serve as an educational coach for many other like-minded Christian schools. Whether it is mentoring principals one-on-one, hosting educational conferences, or going into schools to share with educators my approach to education, revolutionizing Christian education is what I do—it's who I am. I am committed to giving away the tools that I have gained through the years because I know this approach works. This approach to education is what I have used to create a school that started with just twenty-six kids to an increase of over 1200 percent growth in ten years and growing. We now have a three-year waitlist. We start pre-K at age three and parents call us from the hospital after they give birth in order to get them on the waitlist. We had to turn away two hundred and twelve kids this past school year. In the decade that we have been open, our re-enrollment has never been below 97 percent. We have grown exponentially in numbers every single year. Our students test on average 2.5 grade levels above their current grade level on national standardized tests, and we never even mention the word "test" to our students. We don't teach a test, the way we teach just causes them to retain the content. In addition to academic success and growth, our students truly know God and learn the one thing that will sustain them throughout life- how to seek Him. They learn servant leadership and practical ways to be the hands and feet of Christ. Another attribute we are proud of is the return of our educators. We do not have turnover. Most years we have 100 percent of our team return. We have occasionally had a teacher move away or retire, but when people join LCA, they really just don't leave.

Why am I telling you all of this? Not to brag, even though I'm sure right now you think that is what I am doing. I am telling you this to let you know that what I have to say isn't just some fly-by-night thought. This book is filled with box-shattering ideas that actually work. If you are tired of the status quo, or just want some fresh ideas, you've got the right book. Dive in with an open mind.

The heart behind this book comes from a place of talking with people and hearing their idea of what a Christian school is and seeing it with my own eyes. It comes from a place of talking with Christian school leaders who feel lost and not quite sure how to balance the Christian side of their school with the academic side. I see schools that have been doing it the same way for over sixty years and it's just not working. This leads to frustration and tears. I see schools that are run by policies that *do not work*. I hear board members and administrators asking how to keep numbers up. I hear fear in their voices. I see the bubbles that have been created, and kids are shoved in those bubbles to protect them from the outside world. This book is intended to challenge you to *stop*! The days of putting our kids in a bubble and shielding them from the outside world has to stop. The days of giving them a mediocre education just for the sake of it being in a Christian environment has to stop. These kids deserve more! There is a way to give the very best education possible *and* raise an army of world-changers who are encouraged, equipped, and empowered to do the extraordinary. It starts with shattering the box—the old way of doing things—the status quo.

What we are doing is bigger than any one of us. Think about your school … is it the very best school in your region? Really? Is what you offer equipping kids to go out and change the world in whatever field they decide to pursue? Are they prepared academically to be *anything* God has called them to be? Are they prepared spiritually? Are the kids excited to show up every day? Is it fun but also rigorous? Is it engaging in a way that keeps them on their toes wondering what is going to happen next? Are you even excited about what you do? What if I told you that you could answer yes to all of these questions?

The world is a better place because *you are in it.* I know this one thing for sure: **you are here on purpose for a purpose!**

While I know that what we do is ultimately for the kids we teach, I want to challenge you to look deeper than that. I want to challenge you to first look at yourself; to put your oxygen mask on before trying to help someone else.

So often our greatest strengths can also get us in the most trouble if we don't know how to manage them. I guarantee you, if you think about the one thing you are amazing at, you can also think of a way that this quality has gotten you into trouble. I *love* personality tests and strength tests, and because I love learning about others so much, I pretty much love any type of test that allows me to see the way others are wired. I have my team take any and every test imaginable just because the way people are wired intrigues me so much. I am a true believer in the idea that when people know themselves and understand the way they are wired, they can focus more on the things they do well and less on the things they don't.

I'm one of those types of people who likes to believe that everyone is innately good. If you are not one of those types, you're quite possibly rolling your eyes or you've already decided to put this book down, but just bear with me!

I've had conversations with people from all around the world, and anthropology interests me so much! I *enjoy* hearing about what others believe and why they believe that. Travel brings me joy, I love when "worlds" collide, and meeting new people is an absolute passion of mine. I have always been this way and I have a very open mind to the things people believe. In the Christian world, this has gotten me in trouble more often than not, but I love people—I just do. I see value in everyone, and I truly believe that you can learn something from everyone if you stop and truly listen.

I'm wired for conversation. This was a huge problem in school when I was growing up, and my desk was usually the one isolated from the rest of the class (I know we have all had that student in our classroom) and often attached to the teacher's desk. I remember in second grade my desk was moved next to the teacher's desk and I *really* "needed" to tell one of my friends about my new Kaboodle (all of you born in the eighties can appreciate that reference). It was pink and purple. I had painted hearts on this Kaboodle, and I scratched a zig-zag line down the middle of each one so that they would look like "broken hearts." I decided to call it the "Achy Breaky Heart Kaboodle." Wow! I am totally giving my age away. Because of my love of communication, I felt the desperate need to get my friend's attention and I often did. I couldn't quite get to her to tell her of my latest Kaboodle, but I felt so strongly that I *needed* her to see it. That's when the idea came to me. I took my Elmer's glue bottle to the bathroom. I cleaned it thoroughly so that only a white bottle remained. I wrote a note, rolled it up, and stuck it in the glue bottle. For about a week, I used this as a note-passing device, and it worked beautifully! That is, until my teacher took it, because, of course, the lesson we were doing had nothing to do with glue. I was completely busted. This was just one of the countless stories I could tell you about me getting in trouble for my love of talking. I won't even go into the time in seventh grade when I had in-school suspension (for excessive talking) and so I drilled a hole through the divider wall in order to pass a note to the "inmate" to the right of me. Okay, so I know what you are thinking, and it's probably the same thing most of the educators who taught me as a child think: "This person is the principal and co-founder of a school?" Yep. That's me. Who would have known, right? I continued to get in trouble for talking throughout my entire school experience. I was even sent to an alternative school for a week in ninth grade for "excessive classroom disruptions," aka talking. Nothing and no one could get me to stop and sit quietly. I didn't know why, and I certainly didn't view it as a good quality. It was something I wanted so badly to change about myself. I wanted to be able to sit and learn like everyone else—I just couldn't.

My talking habit never seemed to be viewed as a positive. It was only ever an annoyance to others. Phrases like "You would talk to a wall if you were in a room by yourself" were commonly said to me. I never knew that talking could be a strength; I only ever got in trouble for it. For years and years, it was a problem that I just wanted to fix. I am an educator, so believe me, I know that the kid who just won't stop talking can drive an educator absolutely crazy!

I also always knew that I would say whatever was on my mind without thinking of the consequences of my words, and I totally see how that can be a negative.

But what if it's not? What if that child in your class who just can't seem to shut up is wired that way on purpose for a purpose? What if they are called to speak into the lives of others and completely change their lives for the better? What if you were the one who spotted that quality and called it out in them? What would it look like if, for years and years, they had been told that the way they were wired *by God* was wrong because it didn't fit into the cute little box called education that has been set before us, and you decided to shatter that box? That box that is now old and falling apart, but for some reason we keep trying to fit inside of it.

What if you had a quality that you had always viewed as a negative because, somewhere along the way, someone told you it was different and you interpreted that as weird? Or maybe they said it was weird and you believed that lie. What if you started looking at yourself through the filter of God our Father, the one who put that in you, a God who is waiting for you to see the reason for the abnormalities? What if that thing inside you that you think is a major flaw is just the thing that God wants to use to catapult you into a higher calling? I believe it is. I believe that there are things inside of each of us that we have suppressed for far too long. I believe that you were created on purpose for a purpose, and it's way past time to view those qualities as strengths. You add value. *Yes, you.* You have creative ideas. You may lack the boldness to speak them or try them, but I hope that this book inspires you to dig deep and then rise up!

We just have to be aware of our strengths and weaknesses and use them to our advantage and to the advantage of those around us.

Self-awareness is vital. You have to know who you are and who you are not. When people know who they are and they know how they are wired, there is a natural confidence that comes over them. When you know what you bring to the table, you can walk in boldness in that gift. I believe with every fiber of my being that God created us on purpose for a purpose.

If you are a teacher, the kids that you pour your efforts into every day are in your class on purpose for a purpose. They deserve your very best. Shatter the box. Give them your all. Pour from a full cup. Start to see yourself the way

God sees you. You are royalty. You are a child of God. What on earth makes you think you are not worth investing in? If anyone has ever told you or made you feel like you are not worth it, *hear me now*: you are!

If you are an administrator, your team is everything. Give your all to them and help them to see the potential they possess. Encourage them. Equip them, and please, please, please empower them to try. Give them opportunities to be creative, and when they miss the mark—don't freak out. If you do, they won't try again, and oh, what a tragedy that would be. Your success depends on that team of yours, and their success within your organization depends on how much you pour into them and the opportunities you give them. Let them fly! It will blow your mind when you see what they are truly capable of when that old rotten box that you've been trying to fit them into for fear of the unknown is shattered.

I hope this book inspires you and challenges you to get to know yourself. Love yourself. Appreciate the things that make you—you. Embrace the quirky things you do. When you know who you are, you can walk with confidence knowing that you add value.

And then I pray that it inspires you to help those around you to see these things in themselves. My hope is that you will find it inside you to live a life that encourages, equips, and empowers in every area. There is such amazing potential when we unlock these qualities. How amazing would this world be if we each committed to encouraging, equipping, and empowering ourselves and the people we come into contact with every single day? Wow! We could truly change the world.

You want to be a part of revolutionizing Christian education? Let's do it!

Chapter 1

Excellence without Excuses

From the very beginning of LCA, excellence has been at the forefront. Excellence isn't something that just happens one day when you are in a brand-new facility with a full staff to keep everything nice and neat. Excellence is a way of being. Doing things with excellence matters. If you don't treat what you are doing with the utmost excellence, then others simply will not respect it.

Before we opened up to the public, my family had been meeting as a homeschool group in a school setting, and uniform wasn't something that was enforced because it obviously wasn't necessary. When I filed us as a private school and decided to open it up to the public, I made the decision to have uniforms. This was a standard I wanted to set from the very beginning. To almost everyone who had been involved prior to this, this was such a silly thing to establish and enforce. It was literally only twenty-six kids with two adults. While this may have appeared silly to some people, I made the decision and stuck to it. I wasn't viewing this as a school of twenty-six; I was looking ahead to what we were building. Never let where you are lessen the value of where you are going. Do everything as if it were the end result.

A lot of the principals I mentor are put into an environment that they didn't create. A lot of them are in situations that are difficult to navigate because it is hard to change a culture. It may be hard, but you have it in you if you are willing to fight for it. Excellence is something worth fighting for. I challenge you to make the decision not to settle for less than the very best in every single area that you have control over. This is not just for administrators. Make a habit of doing things well in your classroom. From decorations to lessons, give it your all!

Why do these things really matter?

1. Because we are a representation of Christ in education. Everything we do should be done as unto Him. He deserves our best!

2. Because our students deserve the best we have to offer. We are raising up world-changers and in

doing so they need to see excellence modeled in every area. When we do this, they will not settle for less than their best.

We do this in many different ways and have done this at every stage of the school's existence. I am going to give you a few examples of things that work for us. Each school's culture is different, but the following tips can be applied in all environments.

Our awards programs are over-the-top elaborate. Our teachers dress in formals; the students have a red carpet with a separate "celebrity" entrance. We have a full band, lights, stage, and sound generously provided by a state-of-the-art production company. If we had to pay full price for this full-scale awards program, it would cost well over $70,000. When people see our awards programs, they think this is so far out of their reach, but the truth is we were celebrating our students with the utmost excellence long before we were able to provide this type of production for them. From day one, we created programs and had lights (even if the spotlight had to be turned on by hand and held). We celebrated our students' success and made them feel like they were the most incredible students on the planet—because they were! I can't reiterate enough that that excellence has very little to do with resources and budget. Start where you are and continue to raise the bar each year.

Picking up trash off the ground doesn't cost a dollar, but if you do it and have your students do it, a respect for your facility will grow and it will blow your mind. It starts with your team. Do you, as an educator, love and respect your facility? If you don't, no one will.

I'll never forget the day we had a Back to School Family Night. We had jumps, food, drinks, a snow cone truck, etc. We had around 700 people in attendance, and one of the new families asked me if I needed help after the event to pick up the trash on campus. I told them thank you and that I appreciated the offer, but that we wouldn't have trash on the campus when it was over. They laughed until they realized I wasn't joking. I know our families, and I know they love our school. At that same event, I went inside to grab a large trash bag to change out, and by the time I got outside, a dad had taken the trash from that can to the dumpster and changed out the bag. There was not one single piece of trash on our campus following this event, *and* the trash cans that were out there were taken to the school dumpster. Why am I telling you all of this? Because this is not accidental, and this does not just happen. This love and respect for our facility comes from seeing a team who loves and respects our facility. They see teachers picking up trash, and it sparks something in them to do the same. It is a culture that will just become who you are if you set the example.

I remember the time I went to the dentist and the dentist was talking to the hygienist about her recent vacation. The entire visit, they talked about that trip, and I honestly felt invisible. I left that visit and shared this experience with my team. We have always been kind to our students' parents; don't get me wrong. Our parents are absolutely amazing! But this experience at the dentist led to us being very intentional about our interactions. When you are in the carline, this is not the time to visit with the teacher next to you. Face the cars and be ready to greet each person pulling up as if you were waiting for them to arrive. We all know how rushed and stressful mornings can be. This is a time to show parents and students how valuable they are to us. When a parent pulls up and stops to let their child out, greet them and tell them to have a great day. Stop and talk to the child as they are walking toward the door. This is so important. This simple gesture can set the tone of their entire day. Be intentional with those interactions. Please don't have your back to them; be waiting and ready to greet those kids. They are so very valuable, and it doesn't take much to make their day better.

How many times have you heard or said, "This job would be easy if it weren't for parents"? This is a common saying in the education world. I want to challenge you to change this mindset. Parents *are not* the enemy. If you go into it thinking that they are the opposition, they will become the opposition. Include them! Treat them as team members working with you toward a common goal. The more you allow them to be a part of the process and the more communication you have with them, the better it will be. Ultimately, you both want what is best for that child. You have that in common, so start there. They just want to know what is going on and they just want to feel like they are a part of the process. One little side tip I have learned over the years is to keep at-home projects to a minimum. *In house, in house, in house!* Projects should be done in house if at all possible. When doing those projects, invite those parents who want to be involved to help with the projects. This will give those parents that outlet, and those who work full time and are unable to do those types of projects because of their work schedule will love you for it.

Here are a few additional quick tips for your learning environment that we apply and which help us to bring excellence to our school (I asked my team for help on this part, so shout-out to them for helping me think of all the things we do to set a standard of excellence):

– Make an effort to know each student's name. Each student, not just the kids in your class. There is something so powerful about someone hearing their name. It makes them feel valuable. If you know their name, use their name. If you don't know their name, learn it!

– Create moments. If you have an idea that would make a student feel loved and valued, do it! Don't worry about the fact that you didn't do the same thing for everyone. If you do this enough, they will all have those moments throughout their time at the school.

– Set up your classroom in such a way that it feels like an extension of home. We have the amazing opportunity to create a comfortable environment. It doesn't have to look institutional. Do everything you can to make it a place where deep thinking can happen and innovative ideas flow.

– Make an effort to greet everyone with a smile and speak to them. Set this as a standard for your students. If they pass someone in the hallway, they should always acknowledge them. This is something that is taught and modeled.

– Keep things tidy! Before you leave your classroom for any reason, your students should do a rundown of the room and clean up. This takes a minute or less if each student does their part, but it makes such a difference. Everything from the absence of trash on the floor to backpacks hung facing in the same direction sets a standard of excellence.

- Don't use paper on bulletin boards. Flat fitted sheets work great, are just as cheap, and look *so much better*. Pull it extra tight and staple, staple, staple! Trust me on this—so much better than that paper background. People will be singing your bulletin board praises.

- If you put something on the wall, frame it if possible. Frame your alphabet letters if you teach primary kids, and frame all sorts of other things on your walls. Don't just go to School Aides and pick up posters to tape or staple to your wall. This cheapens the look of your space and doesn't set a standard of excellence.

- Cover the cords. We have white walls, so we use Mavalus tape, but any way to keep cords from being exposed and messy will work.

- Smells matter. Keep things smelling nice. On days when you will have visitors at the school, do not cook popcorn or other smelly foods in your classroom. If it burns, the smell makes a terrible first impression.

Now, before you put this book away with the mindset of "This girl is OCD and has lost her mind," hear me out. I am *far* from OCD! At our school we have so much fun, and laughter explodes from our classrooms. We get messy and our classrooms are well lived-in! These are not standards that we put in place to make it feel military-like. In fact, our learning environments are anything but. This level of excellence is intentional. These are standards put in place to ensure the very best quality of education. These cultural norms are such a part of who we are that we don't even realize that it is being done. This is the point.

We are raising up world-changers and, in doing so, everything we do must be intentional. Excellence is a vital part of this for many reasons, but when you value your space, it leads to valuing yourself. Valuing yourself then leads to valuing others. Valuing others is what world-changers do! This is the goal. This is the method to our madness. And it works. Don't believe me? Try it out.

Chapter 2

I Am Not Enough

Now that we have looked at some practical steps to take from an external perspective, let's dive into the heart of it all. You have to look within before you can begin to worry about the external. There is a common word that is used in our culture today …

Enough.

This word is thrown around a lot in our culture today—this idea that no matter what, you are enough. If you breastfeed, you are enough. If you bottle feed, you are enough. If you homeschool, private school, public school, you are enough. Enough. Enough. Enough.

If you don't get dressed for the day, you are enough. If you work, you are enough. If you stay home with your babies, you are enough. The list goes on and on.

The idea behind this is good. It began with great intentions, I am sure. But I am going to go against the popular thing to say and challenge this idea. I am going to say something that is so far from where we are as a culture today and what has become culturally appropriate …

We are not enough!
You are not enough!

This excuse for anything and everything we want to do has to stop! Now, bear with me. I am all about encouraging, equipping, and empowering, so how on earth is it possible that I am starting off in Chapter 2 telling you that you are not enough? Because it is true! I can't read another book that tells me that everything is going to be okay and that if I will just find it within myself to rise up, I am enough and everything will be fine—the idea that everything will be alright if I can just find my inner strength and push forward. We are strong and we are capable, and getting off our couch and taking bold steps of faith is absolutely necessary to be successful, but we are not, nor will we ever be, enough. We weren't created to not need help. We weren't created to run this race alone. Alone, we are not enough.

I have four young children: Cruz, Piper, Beckett, and Nash. I was determined to have four kids in four years and have them all by the age of thirty. Looking back, I realize that this was an insane undertaking, but I absolutely love my kiddos, and although I had to buy diapers and pull-ups for a solid eight years, I wouldn't trade it for anything.

My oldest was a month away from turning five and I was a month away from turning thirty-one when I had my fourth child. It was definitely an "I did it" moment for me. At twenty-five, I began living out my dream as the co-founder and principal of Life Christian Academy. My mom was a retired teacher and had made the decision to homeschool her grandkids and close family friends in a structured school setting when I came to her with the idea to take what she was doing and open it up to the public. My husband had agreed to embrace this idea under one condition: that I convince twenty people to trust us with their children. This was a challenge that I was ready for. I started calling everyone I knew in an attempt to bring my dream to fruition. We spent the summer of 2011 researching, filing what seemed like a million documents, and calling anyone and everyone who might possibly sign up for this. With a retired teacher on board (my mom), I am one hundred percent convinced that this was the *only* reason anyone said yes to me. I was fresh out of college and had very large dreams. After calling more people than I could count, we started the 2011–2012 school year with twenty-six students. We were in shock that this many people had said yes to this crazy dream. I didn't know what I was doing, and "fake it 'til you make it" was the philosophy I would have to live by. My brother and both of my sisters own their own businesses, but it was never the plan for me to own a school—I honestly didn't know that was a thing. Who just decides to open their own school? Apparently, me. I was the sibling who went to college to be a teacher. Never in a million years would I have dreamed that I would one day be an entrepreneur. This idea wasn't on my radar, but I believe that it was always God's plan.

The town I am from only had one option when it came to schools: the public school that was named after the town. That was it, and that was all I had ever known. In the surrounding towns, there were a few church-run options but nothing that even remotely looked like what I dreamt of having. I had a dream to have a place where kids would be seen for who they are. I wanted to create a place full of creativity and excitement. A place where music and dancing were a part of the everyday norm. A school where experiencing learning was an everyday occurrence.

If I were to ask you to think back through your educational experience and tell me a lesson you remember, I am willing to bet that you would never tell me a time when you were told to open your history book and read the chapter on World War II and answer the questions about it at the end. You may tell me about a time when your teacher gave you the opportunity to create a 3D map on the floor in your classroom. We remember experiences, and chances are you have a handful (if you're lucky) of those memories from your entire thirteen years in grade school.

What I dreamed of didn't exist—believe me, I researched to its fullest extent. I wanted a space that created so many experiences that learning just overflowed. A place full of music and creativity. I dreamed of a school where teachers wore costumes and transformed learning spaces regularly. I dreamed of a school that taught outside of the book; a place that shattered the educational status quo. I wanted academic excellence *and* Christ. Put these two things together and there is absolutely no limit to what can be done. There was only one problem: this school I dreamed of didn't exist. I didn't have a model to base it on. I was a twenty-five-year-old girl with big dreams and no possible idea about how to make those dreams come true. It was something I was so passionate about, but as I tried to explain it to people, they would just look at me as if I had lost my mind. "This has never been done because it can't be done" was something that I felt like I was constantly hearing, but I knew it was a God-breathed dream, and I knew that the only way to make people understand was to just do it. Stop talking and get to work.

From day one, adversity hit. When you are trying to do something that looks different, adversity will hit. You have to know that you and your students are worth it. You have to fight for what you believe in; no one will ever believe in it like you do. Go ahead and establish that now.

The first official year of LCA (open to the public), we decided to split the group down the middle. My mom took the younger ones, and I took the older ones. We rented a little Sunday school building for $1 a month and had two classrooms and one toilet. Our playground was a rock parking lot where the kids played capture the flag every single day (imagine the skinned knees), and we were *so proud*! We had no idea what rollercoaster we were getting on, but we trusted God completely.

So there I was, twenty-five years old, principal of a school, starting the whirlwind of this idea of having four kids in four years, and not having a clue what I was doing. I trusted God—trusting God was my only option. I knew that what we were doing was from Him and that He would be faithful to see it through.

If you want to shift the status quo and shatter the box, seek Him. You will need His constant guidance. When you know that you have heard from Him, it makes facing opposition so much easier. When you live your life for an audience of one and you know that you are pleasing Him, nothing else really matters. If God is for you, who can be against you?

The pressure was on! Actual real-life people were trusting me with their most prized possessions—*their children*. My husband often says that I chose the most difficult profession. As we educators all know, the crazy comes out when you are dealing with people's children. Momma bears are no joke, and we all have that in us, so we know it all too well. The reality set in that I was responsible for their education, so letting them down was not an option. I was in a constant state of being pregnant because four in four was something I was absolutely determined to do. I found a way to manage the appearance of pressure. I had to be superwoman (or at least appear to be) and had no other option in my mind. I was enough and that was all there was to it. If I said it enough, it would be true—right? We've all had situations like this in our lives where we just say "I've got this" over and over, doing our very best to convince ourselves that it is true. I bet you are thinking of a time right now. That is exactly where I was. I had signed up for this; it wasn't something I was thrown into. I had done everything in my power to convince everyone around me that I was confident and had it all together. I was strong, confident, and capable. *I was enough!*

Wasn't I?

When reality set in, I actually wasn't sure. I was so young; I had no mentor; I had no clue what went into running a school. My limited experience forced me to start reading. If you are stuck and feel like you are in over your head, I encourage you to lay your pride aside and find a resource. Because I didn't know of anyone else doing what I dreamed of, I started to dive into books on leadership and entrepreneurship. I read every leadership book out there. I pulled from any and every resource imaginable, grasping for something—anything—to help me know what to do during this time. It is amazing what you will do when you become desperate. I pressed into God like never before. I read and read some more. Before this, the only thing I read was fiction books based in the late 1800s. All that was put aside—I needed real help. I was way in over my head and felt so very alone. To the outside world, I was superwoman; I was managing it all. From the outside looking in, I *was* enough; in fact, I was more than enough.

Until I wasn't.

I slowly found myself feeling completely alone. I couldn't reach out to anyone because I didn't have a single person in my life who wasn't directly reliant on me having it all together. Everyone I was close to had kids at the school or taught at the school. My pride was much too strong to allow anyone in. I didn't dare let anyone know that I was struggling.

As we started growing, my friends became my team members. In my mind, my entire world was full of people who depended on me having it all together. I remember counseling other school leaders and telling them, "You have to have it all together! You simply don't have another option, because people are depending on you!" Looking back, I realize how horribly misleading this was, but at the time it was all I knew, and I truly believed it.

Objective: put a smile on and make it all look okay!

The students were fine; in fact, they were excelling academically and spiritually. It wasn't about the quality of education—that was something I knew we had under control. As educators, we give it our all, right? The rest of the world can be collapsing around us, but we will pull through for our students. We are resilient in this way.

It wasn't about the education side of things; it was about my quality of life. It was about me pouring from an empty cup over and over again. I was depleted and didn't know how much more I had in me. Sound familiar? I know what it is like to feel depleted. I know that feeling of exhaustion that most educators feel on a daily basis. I know the amazement that we feel when we make it through another day of teaching when we didn't think we had it in us. I lived it, and I found an answer to living this way. I am on the other side of this and I want to help pull you out as well. There is hope. There is rest. There is joy. If I can find it, you can too! Your students deserve to find this, but more than that, you deserve to find it.

I was in this place of feeling alone but not able to show weakness because everyone around me was trusting that I knew what I was doing. I looked for resources or *anyone* who had started a school that I could go to for guidance, and I found nothing. The more I looked, the more alone I felt. How could I manage all of these things? What had I signed up for? What was I thinking? Every leadership book I read said to find someone a few steps ahead of you and go to them for guidance, but this didn't exist. Sure, I didn't invent private schools, but everything I found was church run or had been around so long that the original founders were no longer alive.

There would be days when I was on cloud nine, feeling like I was living out my purpose, and Rick Warren didn't have anything on me. Put me in my classroom with those amazing children, and the worries of the world would vanish. Purpose-driven life—check. I bet you could say the same. Those days when you have an incredible lesson to teach and you know your students will love it. You wake up giddy about it and excited about seeing their faces light up. These are the best days!

And then there were days when adversity would hit, my character was questioned, my motives were not interpreted correctly, and I just wanted to close the doors and walk away. Have you experienced this? Maybe you had an awesome idea and couldn't wait to share it with your admin or your board, only to be shut down. Maybe you created an incredible lesson and the teacher across the hall rolled her eyes or made a rude comment that came from her own insecurities but made you feel like crap. Perhaps this has happened to you so many times that you quit trying. Perhaps you're reading this book thinking, "Sure it all sounds great, but you don't know my school board. You don't know how much they love that old crusty box." I hear you. But stick with me. Don't give up; please don't give up! You and your students depend on you.

"Just keep swimming" was the only thing I knew to do. I knew God's hand was on this dream; I knew He was with me, so I just had to keep swimming. But for how long? I felt like I was drowning. I felt like I was alone in the middle of the ocean running out of strength.

No matter what sort of day it was, there was one thing that was constant—this overwhelming feeling that … *I was never enough.*

I didn't have enough time. I didn't have enough money. I didn't have enough of me to go around. I had a husband, kids, staff, students, parents (both mine and those of my students), and what seemed like a million other things pulling me in a million different directions. On top of all of that, I had recently had two miscarriages. I told no one but my husband about them because in my mind that made me weak and would make people feel sorry for me. So, so crazy, I know! I showed up at work the day after one of my miscarriages and put a smile on like nothing was wrong, but inside I was at breaking point. We had around fifty students enrolled in the academy at the time, and we were at full capacity in the building we were renting. We had opened up registration in February of that school year and had 130 new students apply. How was this even possible? This was huge! But why wasn't I more excited? From an outside standpoint, the school (my dream) was absolutely thriving, but inside I wasn't. I was barely treading water.

Women are strong—no doubt about it! But somewhere along the way we have traded this idea of being independent and strong for trying to be invincible with something to prove. We are not! We will break! You know why? You guessed it … because we are not enough.

I realized this when I finally hit my breaking point. In an attempt to escape the reality of the stress, I disconnected from my kids, my husband, my job, and my friends. I still went through the motions, but inside I was broken and starving for any escape. I put so many things over my family and found myself in a broken state of mind. The feeling of "having to have it all together" had left me absolutely broken. It took me nearly losing it all and nearly walking away from it all to remind me that I am not enough and *that is the way it's supposed to be*! I am not enough and that is *okay*!

Wait—what? Yep, you read that correctly!

We were never created to be enough. I am not enough, you are not enough, nor will any of us ever be enough. We need to shift our focus from this mindset that we are enough … *We aren't, but God is!*

Our identity has to be found in Him. We have to know that we are fully known and loved by Him. He cares about the details, and where He guides, He provides.

But how? How can we possibly trust God when life gets crazy? How can we trust God through the chaos of life? Life is hard. I have come to realize that we are either going through something hard, coming out of something hard, or about to go into something hard. That is just the cycle of life. So how? How can we fully trust Him? Not in a Sunday-school, I-know-this-is-what-I-am-supposed-to-say-so-I-will-say-I-trust-Him sort of way. How can we *really* trust Him? The answer is going to sound so elementary, but it's the answer, nonetheless. We trust Him the same way we trust anyone.

We have to know Him.

Chapter 3

Knowing and Trusting God

Think about your life. How well do you know God? How often does He speak to you? When things get crazy, do you truly trust that it is all going to work out because you know that God works all things together for the good of those who love Him? Or is this just something we've learned to say because it sounds good? How can we expect to truly raise up world-changers to know and trust God if we don't? I am assuming that if you are reading this book, you would label yourself a Christian; I am not talking about that label. I am talking about truly trusting God when things are hard.

To trust God on the mountain is easy. To trust Him in the deepest valley when your world is crumbling to pieces—that's when God becomes real. That's when the opportunity to truly trust God comes in.

Knowing God is the *only* way we can walk boldly, knowing that no matter how hard life gets, He is enough. Knowing God is the only way to walk with the confidence that we don't have to be enough. Knowing God is really the only way to trust Him, and the only way to really know God and trust Him is to spend time with Him.

This seems like a very obvious thing to say, but it's really not. You know how I know this? Because I was raised in church; my mom led children's church my entire life; I was at church every time the doors were opened; I went to every youth event; I was a rainbow, daisy, prim, and star in Missionettes (my Assembly of God people will get that reference); in college I did an internship at my church; I was on staff at that same church; I then went on to Bible college. All this time, I served God and I prayed. I knew He was real and I believed in Him, but I didn't trust Him completely … at least, not yet. I thought I did, but when life truly gets bad, you really find out what you are made of. When you take a real look at yourself without any filter, it's really ugly, and when you do this, you truly realize your need for Him. When you truly self-evaluate, you will see your deep need for a relationship with the Father. "Deep cries out to deep"; when you get to a true understanding of your need for Him, the deepest parts of you will cry out to the deepest parts of Him. We have to long to know Him deeply and intimately. You want to thrive in life? Dive deep into a relationship with Him. Hold nothing back. Tap into all He has for you. We have access to blessings that we don't walk in because we won't give all of ourselves and our will to Him.

I was in tenth grade the first time I truly encountered God. I went through a dark time in high school. It started with a boy, as all great high school stories do. What began with me feeling rejected quickly grew into something much deeper. Rejection I had faced as a younger child resurfaced, and I was much too young to understand my emotions and how to deal with them. Why wasn't I enough? Depression took over.

Side note: Please don't discredit a student's or your own child's depression, even if it starts with something seemingly insignificant. The enemy is real, and depression is real. For my junior high and high school teachers, believe me, I know hearing that a child has suicidal thoughts is common, but *never, ever* take it lightly. Suicide is at an all-time high, as you know, so please don't discredit a child whom you are worried about.

Okay, back to my story … I had gotten to a place of such dark depression. I would wear the same Gap hoodie every day, I didn't shower (I'm sure that hoodie smelled great), I didn't care about school, my grades suffered, I even switched schools for a semester. I had allowed the lies of the enemy to make me feel worthless. What started as something small had grown in my mind into something that was no longer about any one thing. It was about my identity. When depression truly takes over, all rational thinking goes out of the window. After a while, my body began to react to the way I was treating it, and I got sick and very weak over the course of six months. One rainy afternoon I went into my backyard. I was sick, weak, depressed, and by this point I didn't even know what I was depressed about. I just was. It wasn't one thing; it was my life. I was just tired of living it. My dad was working on the guest house and had left his tools outside. I sat in the backyard, in the pouring rain, thinking about which tool I could use to take my life. Next to his toolbox was a pair of hedge trimmers. I picked them up and rocked back and forth as I sat on the ground crying, out of control. In that moment, I cried out to God from a place of desperation— true desperation. I begged Him to show up. I yelled out to Him, "Where are you? Are you even real? Do you even care?" I remember closing my eyes, still rocking back and forth, and a slideshow began to play in my mind. I remember it vividly. Pictures of my childhood; pictures of things I had gone through in my life; times I had cried myself to sleep after my grandmother, whom I loved more than anything, had passed away; times when I was broken, hurting, scared, rejected, or sad. Some of the greatest times in my life were projected in my mind as well. Moments of absolute brokenness and moments of pure joy. It was a slideshow of my life and every picture had two things in common: I was there, and Jesus was there. This warmth came over me and, in that moment, I knew He loved me, I knew He cared about the details, and I knew He was there. It was the first time in my life that I truly experienced His presence. There was no one who could ever convince me that God wasn't real or that He didn't care. He met me there in the pouring rain. This broken teenager whom He gave His life for. I cried out and my amazing heavenly Father wrapped His loving arms around me in an almost tangible way.

In that moment, I gave my life to God. I knew that He was real. I had grown up knowing about Him. I knew all of the surface-level things. I had learned the books of the Bible at four years old, but it was in that moment that I went from knowing of Him to knowing Him.

My story of salvation is a beautiful story, and I know God allowed me to walk through that so that I could one day see a greasy-haired teenager wearing a hoodie (as most teenagers do, no matter how hot it is outside), looking like the weight of the world is on their shoulders, and see them for who they are inside and who they are going to be. I know He works all things for the good of those who love Him and who are called according to His purpose. He is true to His word, and He makes beauty from ashes.

I think that for a lot of us, this is where our testimony ends. It's like a Hallmark movie; it's all about the journey to find love, then roll the credits. But this is not my testimony. This is my story of salvation. This is my story of finding God.

But what about trusting Him?

To trust someone, you have to know them. And to know someone, you have to spend time with them. I can know that a chair will hold me up, but it isn't until I sit in that chair that I truly trust it. It's not always easy to trust someone, even God. One thing I know for sure is that the more I get to know Him, the more I trust Him. We have to be intentional about spending time in His Word; we have to spend time in prayer; we have to spend time just being still and listening for His voice. He is there. He is just waiting for us to draw near to Him. You can't encourage yourself enough. There aren't enough pep talks, TED

Talks, podcasts, motivational messages, memes, or quotes to encourage you.

Until we fully come to the realization that we are not enough and we will never be enough, we will never be able to be fulfilled. We have to stop trying to do it with our own strength. We have to not only know God but trust Him with our lives. We have to trust His Word when it says in Jeremiah 29:11 that He knows the plans He has for us. They are plans to prosper and not harm us, plans to give us a future and a hope.

We have to do as it says in 1 Samuel 30:6 and encourage ourselves **in the Lord**. He is our strength. He is our provider. He is our Father. *He is enough.* He gives us what we need! He is our source of encouragement. We are His children and we make Him so proud. He has set up a plan for our lives, and I truly believe He wants us to live a life encouraged and full of joy. He has set out such a clear plan to living out a joyful life.

I know that as an educator, you encourage students every day. Chances are, you encourage your students, your co-workers, your spouse, your kids, and everyone in between; it's the nature of an educator to do so. But please hear me; encourage yourself first. Please don't try to pour from an empty cup. Please put on your oxygen mask first before trying to help someone else. Your long-term success and fulfillment depend on it! Don't take this lightly.

You will never live out your full potential if you don't take care of *you*.

You are worth it. You really, really are! And anyone or anything that makes you believe otherwise needs to go. I don't care if it's a relative or a friend you have had since you were three … get rid of the negative voices tearing you down. You are so much better than that, and if you think you can encourage yourself enough with those negative voices in your head … you are wrong! Ships don't sink because of the water around them; ships sink because of the water that gets into them. Don't let the negative voices around you get inside you. Distance yourself from negativity. Surround yourself with people who believe in you. They are out there. Don't settle for anything less!

Chapter 4

Speak Life

I'll never forget the day I walked into Tiger Stadium for the first time. I was eighteen years old, and I had been dreaming of the day that I would be a student at Louisiana State University for as long as I could remember. I dreamed of going to school there, not for the academics or the beautiful oak-tree-covered campus. I dreamed of LSU football. I dreamed of being a Tiger and bleeding purple and gold. In the state of Louisiana, LSU is the only school that matters. This is what dreams are made of. When the state really needs to get their point across, they call on the LSU head football coach to give a public statement because they know people will listen to him more than they will listen to the governor or any other politician. This is not a joke, although I wish it were.

51

The day had finally come. The fall air was crisp, and I had been up for what seemed like hours. We loaded up our ice chests and tents, made a stop by Raising Cane's to pick up a tailgate package, and headed over to campus. The smell of everything from jambalaya to gumbo cooking was invigorating. The music was loud. Purple and gold was all you could see in every direction. In my opinion, you haven't lived until you have been tailgating on LSU's campus. There is a feeling of family that is contagious. If you are wearing LSU attire, you are a part of this gigantic, crazy, loud, unorthodox family. There isn't a tent that won't welcome you in. I was eighteen years old and I had heard about this, but I never could've imagined how invigorating this experience truly was. We met up with some friends and I did my best to take in every single moment. We ate and laughed, played games, walked over to watch the Golden Band from Tiger Land lead the march down Victory Hill followed by the coaches and players all dressed in suits down to the stadium. There were so many people, the energy was overwhelming. It was at this moment that I knew I was a Tiger! Once the band and the players marched down, it was time to go inside the stadium. I was giddy with excitement. I had dreamed of *this moment* for as long as I could remember. I was a small-town girl and

I had never experienced anything even close to this. Was this real life? I was about to walk into Death Valley, and I was 100 percent freaking out!

My roommate in college knew someone who did recruiting, so we were able to go in through the entrance where they bring recruits. As we entered, we walked past the 2003 National Championship trophy the team had won the year prior. It was in a glass case, and it was unreal to be that close to it. We walked through the hallway and saw helmets from what looked to be every NFL team in existence. It was showcasing all the LSU athletes who had gone on to play in the NFL. We continued to walk until we came to the doors that would lead us into the stadium.

Then it happened. They opened the double doors and the most incredible sight I had ever seen was in front of me. The lights were brighter than anything I had ever seen (and I thought Times Square in New York was bright). A hundred thousand fans were chanting in unison, the Golden Band from Tiger Land was playing, and it was jaw-dropping! The energy was unlike anything I had ever experienced. The stadium held my entire hometown's population *times twenty-five*. It was in that moment that I truly fell in love with college football, and I knew that I was an LSU Tiger through and through. There was absolutely no turning back, and there was no way anyone could or would ever convince me that a better team existed. If they thought their stadium was better, it was simply because they had never been to a Saturday night in Death Valley.

Y'all, I know this is a football game and you may be thinking that I am a little too excited about that moment, but please don't tell me to calm down! If you've ever been to a sporting event even close to this, you know the feeling I am referring to. The feeling of energy, the feeling of passion. When the opposing team is given a choice, I can guarantee you they would *never* choose to play toward the student section (at least not in Tiger Stadium). This section is *loud*! And when I say loud, I mean really loud! They yell at the opposing team, and anyone who comes near a Tiger fan wearing an opposing team's colors is very quickly referred to as "Tiger Bait." You know this because this is what us Tiger fans yell repeatedly to anyone and everyone who crosses our path. The energy is high, and, in my opinion, there is no place on earth like it. There is, however, one type of person who doesn't enjoy a Saturday night in Death Valley, and that is a player on the opposing team.

In Louisiana, we are known for our southern hospitality, but when it comes to passion for our Tigers … not so much! We are passionate, we are loud, and, I hate to admit it, but words of affirmation is not our number one love language on a Saturday night. All in fun, of course, but research shows that fans truly do have an impact on the game.

If you are a sports fan, you've seen the impact fans have on a team's performance. If you are an athlete, then you've more than likely experienced it first-hand. Not only is the noise a distraction, but athletes of all sports will tell you that heckling and booing can get in your head and impact your performance. Some use the negativity to push them to perform better, and some get discouraged by it, but either way, players are impacted by both positive and negative fan participation. Author Carl Deuker says, "Games are lost and won in your mind as much as they are on the field." I'm not an athlete, but I think the energy felt at sporting events has proven this to be true. Cheering has the ability to make athletes feel like someone believes in them. Booing, however, can have the opposite effect.

Isn't life just like this?

Think through your life. I guarantee you can remember a time when someone told you something that cut deep. A moment where truth was twisted or a time when the negative side of your wiring was used against you to hurt you. Perhaps it wasn't just one moment; perhaps it was years and years of being told you don't have value. Maybe it came from your parents or possibly a teacher. I've heard stories of coaches telling their players that they don't have what it takes. Those moments stick with us. Those words cut deep and cause pain that doesn't just go away.

On the other hand, I am sure we can all think of a time when someone somewhere along the way spoke life over us. Just one small compliment or one "I believe in you" can make you feel like you can conquer the world. When we look through our lives and think of the people who spoke positivity into our lives, we think back on them with such fondness. Those words stick.

As an educator, we get the amazing opportunity of speaking into the lives of young people every day. We get to see those "aha" moments and encourage our students to stretch themselves even more. Educators don't always get to see the fruit of their hard work, but sometimes we get a glimpse of the lasting impact our words can have. We have such a unique opportunity to help mold young people into the people they will become. It really doesn't matter what age you teach; you have the potential to make someone feel like they can do anything they set their mind to or make them feel like they don't have what it takes.

Although I hope none of us would ever speak negativity into the life of a child intentionally, we have to be careful about what we speak over the students God has entrusted to us. Guard your words. Search for positive things to say. You may be the only positive voice in their life. You may be the only one who sees the way that child is wired and sees the potential that holds. I challenge you to be that voice. Build them up. Be *that* educator.

At our school, we have the most amazing team, and to begin this school year I hired someone my mom had taught in kindergarten. He sent me a text that said, "Wait! Is Carolyn your mom?" When I replied that she was, he was so excited. He told me how she had been his teacher in kindergarten and that when he was in her class, she awarded him Citizen of the Week six times. I laughed as he was telling me this because all of this happened when he was five years old, but it brought back such fond memories that helped mold him into the person he is today and, all of a sudden, he felt like he was five again. What a powerful thought. The ways you reward your students for making good choices even at five years old matters. Every single moment you have with your students matters. Don't waste them. Make the choice to encourage your students and build them up.

I am an educator through and through. I was one of those kids who would line up the stuffed animals in my bedroom and teach them whatever lesson I had learned that day. I love to teach. If you were to ask any of my current or former students to tell you the one thing I say to them more than anything else … they would easily answer, "Speak life." This phrase comes from Proverbs 18:21, "The tongue has the power of life and death."

This is what is often referred to in the Christian world as a "life verse." It is part of my make-up. When I have the opportunity to speak life over someone, it truly brings me joy. When we choose to speak life over others, it sparks something in them that changes things. One activity I do with my students each year is an activity where we write the child's name on a sheet of paper. (We will usually incorporate it into a lesson on adjectives.) They then pass that sheet of paper around the room, and each person writes one positive thing about that child. This is always such a fun lesson, and it is something that our students cling to. Words have power, and this lesson is one that the kids truly enjoy.

As an adult, it's not quite as easy to get these "words of affirmation." I am sure that if you wrote your name on a sheet of paper at a dinner party and passed it around, you would probably not get the same results. Why is it that it's almost become "awkward" to tell others how amazing they are? Pay attention next time you are listening to someone talk about one of their accomplishments. I guarantee that in some way they will downplay it, and if someone doesn't, they are viewed as arrogant and self-absorbed. Why is this?

I am in a small group with a team of amazing women who put on an event each year called Free to be Real. It is all about being authentic and transparent. We had a night when our leader would call out our name and everyone in the room would start saying the things they think about that person. Our leader said "Stefanee" and the words began …

"Driven" from one precious friend. "Motivated" from another. "Leader" from another. "Trailblazer" came from another in the back of the room. "Authentic" was spoken. The list went on and on, then, when the words began to settle, she called the name of another lady in the room. We continued around the room until all the names had been called. When we were done, she asked us to describe what we thought about it. The main adjective used to describe this experience was "uncomfortable." It's great to hear these words spoken over our lives, but it's become so uncommon and so out of the ordinary that we almost cringe when people speak life over us.

How often do we respond to a compliment with a negative? Someone tells us, "Wow! I love your hair!" We respond, "Oh my gosh, it's such a mess." instead of just saying a simple thank you. It's become a cultural norm to downplay the positive. Why has the idea of being humble gotten so twisted that we don't feel like we can think we are awesome or truly believe that other people think we are?

Although this activity was "uncomfortable," there wasn't a single woman in that room who hated it. In fact, when it was over, we all discussed how uncomfortable it was but how we wished we had recorded the words spoken over us because they were so refreshing to hear.

Our words have power. My friends, let's rise up and use the power of our words to encourage those God has placed in our lives! Let's use this ability that we have to build up those who are having a rough day. To tell the mom in the grocery store with her screaming kids, "You're doing a great job!" How about that teacher across the hall who drives you crazy because she is always late for duty? Or the teacher who goes above and beyond and "makes you look bad"? What if you told her how incredible she was instead of rolling your eyes when her bulletin board looks so much better than yours? It sounds so simple and yet it is so uncommon. We all know words have power, so let's use this amazing power that we have. It doesn't cost us a thing to encourage others, but you can't put a price tag on the value it adds to the lives of those around us. Like it or not, we need each other, and we are better together. Let's choose to speak life over the people in our lives. Let's never forget that life and death are in the power of the tongue.

Chapter 5

Better Together

I went through so many years feeling like I had to do it alone. I thought I had to figure it out alone and I had no other choice. This goes against everything the Word of God teaches us. God wants to have communion with us, but he also wants us to have communion with one another. God never intended that we would do life alone. Do you currently feel this way? Do you feel alone? Maybe it is by choice, but maybe it is deeper than that. If you are surrounded by a solid group of friends who build you up and encourage you, you can attest to the fact that it makes life so much better. I went through years of surface-level relationships; a "trust no one" mentality felt like survival mode for me. I truly thought it was necessary. Maybe you are like this. Maybe you have made the decision to put up walls because of pain from the past. Maybe you think this is the best way to avoid pain again; I need to tell you that this is simply not true.

This was revolutionary to me. Of course, it doesn't seem revolutionary or life-changing. It seems like common sense, but women do this all the time. We feel the need to do life alone. Even in a room full of people, we rarely trust others. Why? Perhaps we have been hurt by others in the past. Women can be mean. People can be mean. When we go through life with our guard up, we feel like no one can hurt us. We have this false sense of confidence that we will never be hurt again if we keep these walls around our hearts. But this simply isn't the truth. People are going to fail us, but living a life without trusting others is a miserable life. Trust me, I have been there and done that! Let's make the choice to open up our hearts to trust others.

Is this difficult to do? Absolutely.

Will we be hurt again? One hundred percent.

But we will find so much joy in doing life with other believers. Iron sharpens iron. It has taken me thirty-four years to find "my people," and I know that they are there for me through it all. My natural tendency when I am having a rough day is to isolate myself. I tend to just put on a brave face and pretend to have it all together. I have learned now that if I don't at least let "my people" know that I am having a bad day, they will be at my doorstep ringing the doorbell with a pint of ice cream or chips and salsa, ready to do nothing more than sit if that is all I need. There have been times when I have received a phone call with terrible news on the other end, and my shopping cart was left in the middle of the store because one of "my people" got terrible news that they couldn't process alone and I needed to get to them. I know they have my back.

They aren't people who just say what I want to hear. They speak life over me and celebrate me like no one else, but they will also speak truth in my life when I am making a poor decision. I know they will call me out when I am wrong, and I have learned to put my pride aside and hear them because I know it comes from a place of love. I know that when it comes time for me to have a hard conversation with them about a dumb decision they are making, they will hear my heart as well. I know they will let me sulk alone if I ask them to just give me time, and I know they will tell me to get up and get dressed when I've had a pity party that is lasting too long. They know me, and I know them. I have driven into their driveway crying my eyes out, sent a text to ask them to come outside, and sat with them for hours, talking and praying about the burdens of life.

I am telling you ...

... *you need people!*

We are better together! I can't tell you how many women I talk to on a regular basis who tell me how alone they feel. I have been there. If this is you, believe me, I know what that feels like. I remember being in college, praying and crying out to God to send me just one girl friend. I just wanted one person. The people in my life today have been prayed for. If you are needing and longing for "your people," I challenge you to pray for them, then reach out! Find people whom you feel like you could get along with, and ask them to lunch. I have done this countless times and no one has ever said no. People are genuinely good and kind—seek them out! I have gone through life feeling like I had to handle it on my own. When I realized that God created us for community and began to fervently pray for that community, He gave it to me. He cares about the details, y'all. He cares and He wants to make His children happy. If you have kids, don't you want what is best for them? Don't you want them to live a fulfilled life? Jesus wants us to live a fulfilled life more than we do. He wants us to trust each other.

Will we be hurt? Yep.

Will we want to give up on relationships? Absolutely.

But relationships are worth it! Knowing people love you *no matter what* is an unbelievable thing. Finding "your people" is beautiful. Try it! Pray for it if you don't have this. And if you do, hold on to them for dear life. The enemy hates it when iron sharpens iron. He knows we are stronger and better together. But we have a Father who says we were made to trust in Him and have relationships with one another. We are not enough, but with Him and through positive, life-giving relationships we are overcomers. You want to live a life encouraged? Come to the place where you care enough about yourself that you encourage yourself in the Lord and allow others to encourage you. Try it! I dare you.

Let's make a choice to be a light in the darkness. Let's choose to wake up each day and tell ourselves how amazing we are because we are children of the King, and then go out and speak life over those we encounter on a daily basis. It doesn't take much to make someone's day better; it simply takes us slowing down long enough to notice the good in others.

Let's decide to be the one who makes someone feel like they can conquer the world. You don't know how many people around you are just treading water—they can't even swim anymore. One word of encouragement from you could shift the trajectory of their life. Yes, it's that important. Yes, your words have that much power.

And then let's slow down long enough to encourage our students. Covering content is very important, but we all know relationships are much more valuable. **Connections** are more valuable than **content**! Please don't ever lose sight of that. They do not care how much you know until they know how much you care, so care first! Let's tell the student who drives you crazy because they never have their homework how amazing they are. One practical thing I like to do is to have a roster on a clipboard. Throughout the week I try to say one positive thing to each child in my class and check them off as I have done it. I know it sounds so simple, but if you do this you will start to notice those about whom you have a harder time thinking of something positive to say; those are the ones who need your encouragement the most. The ones in the middle who don't draw a lot of attention are often the ones who are overlooked, and one word from you could make all the difference.

Find good things about them. Get to know them— really know them. What are their interests? Sit with them at lunch instead of with that group of teachers. It truly doesn't take much to encourage others. It takes such a small amount of effort, but I guarantee you, that small act can change someone's entire world. Take time to get to know the kids in your classroom.

Make it your mission to truly see each child. What makes them special? God has wired every person differently; as educators it's our job to discover gifts and **call them out**.

I was giving a tour of our school and I asked some parents to tell me about their child, as I always do. They were telling me things about her, and then they began to tell me that she tends to get in trouble because she is very meticulous. They said that her current teacher was constantly telling her to hurry up with her work and to just pick an answer and move on. I know we have all had students in our class that we can relate this child to. As they were telling me this, I stopped them and told the little girl about what a gift that was. I then explained to them that attention to detail is a God-given gift that not everyone has. I am someone who doesn't have this gift, and I often wish I could focus on things more clearly. I went on to explain to her parents that if organization and taking time to do things correctly is a gift she has, then we can use that as a starting point to help develop that gift. In a classroom setting, this might involve telling her that if she can complete her work, we can give her a job organizing the library, since she is so good at organization. This will push her to complete her work *and* give her the outlet she is needing to use the gift she has.

When we start to focus on the things that make the people in our lives different (whether a student or someone else) as gifts from God, we can speak life into that. We can encourage them to use those gifts. Chances are, the things that make them different are the things they like least about themselves, because what people don't understand about others they tend to view as weird. Let's open our eyes to see the differences in people as gifts, and when we see those gifts, let's encourage each other by calling them out. What would it look like if each teacher in your school started encouraging the people around them? You can be the spark that ignites that fire.

I encourage you to slow down and look for ways to encourage your co-workers and your students. Find something, anything, to build up those around you. There is good to be found and encouragement to be given. Be the one! Be the change you want to see in your school.

Decide here and now to be the one who makes someone else feel better about themselves. Let's build up those around us and never be known as the one who tore someone down.

Chapter 6

Praying the Word

I was sixteen years old, sitting on a pew near the back of the church at a women's event. The speaker that night was sharing her story. I have always loved to hear others share their stories, and this night was no different. I was listening to her tell how she had lost her son in a tragic accident when he was in his twenties. She talked about the devastation she felt, and although I didn't have children yet, I knew that the sadness she must have felt must have been unlike any other pain on this earth. I heard her tell how she went into a time of depression and that the only way she got through it was through her husband being a constant support (even through his own pain) and through the strength she found in God.

Growing up as a member of the church, I had heard countless messages preached, but I had never heard what she went on to say. There was something about the practical application of what she said that day that stuck with me and changed my prayer life in such a powerful way. She went through, step by step, how she prayed the Word of God over her life. She talked about the power that comes when you do this. This was new for me, and I was so interested to learn all about this power that we, as children of God, have access to. I had always prayed, but I had never prayed scripture over my life. She went through Ephesians 6:10–18 and it went something like this:

God, help me to be strong in you and in your mighty power. Right now, I am putting on your full armor, so that I can take my stand against the devil's schemes. I know my struggle is not against flesh and blood but against the rulers, against the authorities, against the powers of this dark world, and against the spiritual forces of evil in the heavenly realms. Therefore, I am putting on the full armor of God, so that I will be able to stand my ground, and after I have done everything, God, I will stand. I will stand firm with the belt of truth buckled around my waist, with the breastplate of righteousness in place, and with my feet fitted with the readiness that comes from the gospel of peace. God, I take up the shield of faith, with which I can extinguish all the flaming arrows of the evil one. I am putting on the helmet of salvation and the sword of the Spirit, which is the word of God. I will be alert and always keep praying.

I went home that night and looked up that very scripture. I started there. Exactly as she had done, I began to pray this over my life each day. I was equipping myself by putting on the armor of God, and I was also learning a very powerful life skill—praying the Word of God over my life.

As time went on, I added to this prayer. I began to read the Bible in a fresh new way. I began to apply it to my life. I began to pray it over my life. "In the beginning was the Word, and the Word was with God, and the *word was God*" (John 1:1). The Bible is literally the living, breathing Word of God, and it is tangible. It is the only tangible form of God, and it is available to us. Have you ever really thought about that? We have access to the living, breathing Word of God. Every answer you could ever need is in that book. We have the answer sitting there, but we, as a whole, take it for granted. Why do we sit and wonder what to do and how to face the tests of life when we have the answer sitting there collecting dust?

We have already established that our words have power, but the power of speaking the Word of God over our lives is unlike anything we could ever imagine.

We are God's children, and when His children step into the authority given to them by their heavenly Father, *it is powerful*. If we are going to talk about equipping ourselves to face the challenges that life throws at us, we have to talk about the Word of God. The Word of God is the sword of the spirit. It is our weapon. Prayer is important and worship is important, but the Word of God is the actual weapon we are instructed to use to stand against the enemy. There isn't a question that can't be found in His Word. There is nothing new under the sun, and the Bible covers it all. Again, trusting God is a process, and in order to trust someone, we have to know them. The Word of God is God.

You want to know God? Read His Word.

You want to be equipped to face anything life throws at you? Read His Word.

You want to know what to do in any given situation? Read His Word.

It is the answer to everything. It paints a picture of the character of Christ. It shows His love, mercy, and justice. It shows us why we should fear Him, respect Him, honor Him, and seek Him. It shows us what's right and what is wrong.

By nature, I am gray. There are black-and-white people out there and, to be honest, most educators are black and white (which always made me feel very out of place in the education field), but I am gray. By saying this, I mean that everything is situational in my mind. My brain thinks that there are always exceptions to every rule. On my strength-finder assessment, discipline is number 34 of 34 for me (we can all laugh at the irony that I am a principal). So it's very easy for me to see situations and want to make exceptions. God, however, is not gray. The Word of God is not gray. The Word of God is *black and white*, and every question we have has an answer that can be found in those pages. It may not be the answer we want to hear, but it is there, and it is the truth, nonetheless.

A while back, there was a Twitter feud between Popeyes and Chick-fil-A. I'm sure we all remember this and have an opinion on which is better. Popeyes came out with a new chicken sandwich and someone said it was better than Chick-fil-A. Well, it went viral and the feud was on. All of a sudden, the to-go line at every Popeyes in the country was so long it was in the street. They were selling out of chicken. Signs were going up on their windows that read, "Sorry, we are out of chicken sandwiches. Be back soon!" It was hilarious to watch. I took my eighth-grade writing class on a "field trip" to both fast food chains, and they had to choose a side, create a PowerPoint, and debate which was better. I tried the new sandwich and it was delicious, but as I told you in the introduction to this book, I am obsessed with studying why things are the way they are. I knew there had to be more to the story. A sandwich just can't be that good. I tasted it and it was good, but there had to be more to it. I started digging. It didn't take me long to find the story that answered my question. A small restaurant was selling Popeyes chicken but not telling their customers that it was from Popeyes. Every day, the owner of this restaurant would go to Popeyes and purchase chicken, bring it back to her restaurant and sell it. One day, a customer saw her coming into the restaurant with the chicken; he snapped a picture and posted it online. Popeyes heard about the restaurant, and instead of suing or being ugly, they decided to offer the restaurant owner the opportunity to do an exclusive early release of their new sandwich one week before Popeyes would have it available in their chains nationwide. People do not know this story; this is not the reason people think they are flocking to Popeyes, but I dare say—it is. This is a principle that could be taken from so many scriptures in the Bible.

Reap and you will sow.

God's ways are perfect, and blessings follow those who do things according to the Word of God.

Give and it will be given unto you, pressed down, shaken together, and running over (Luke 6:38).

Whether or not they realize it, because their offering lined up with a Biblical principle, their act of giving was blessed.

When we study the Word of God and we know what it says, we can operate in this manner in every area of our lives. God's Word does not lie.

The same person who gave her testimony and unknowingly taught me about praying the Word of God over my life crossed my path when I was in my thirties and in a season when I needed big, crazy faith for a new facility for the school because we had outgrown our space ... again. We had lunch, and she began to tell me about faith—big faith. She told me that when we pray the Bible over our lives, we should say it as if it is done. "God, you said this, I didn't. I know you do not lie, and so I believe if you did it for them that you will do it for me."

We can know that we are blessed and highly favored.

We can walk in authority.

We can truly be equipped to face each day.

If you haven't stepped into the power that comes when you pray the Word of God over your life, I challenge you to do so. Start small, but start. And maybe you do this already. I challenge you to dive in deeper. Get to know God even more. Seek and you will find; knock and the door will be opened.

The Bible tells us that we are heirs. We are a royal priesthood. It tells us that Jesus has given us permission to use His name when we approach the throne of God. When you really grab hold of the things that the Bible says about you, it is a game-changer. Worried about sickness? Pray Psalm 91 over your life: "No plague will come near my dwelling" or "by His stripes I am healed." We have to equip ourselves with the Word of God. There is no more powerful tool out there. It is our weapon. It is our sword.

Equipping yourself with the Word of God changes things. It is truly revolutionary! You can't equip your students if you haven't first equipped yourself. There is power in praying the Word of God over your life. Don't settle for mediocre Christianity. Don't settle for living inside the box you were raised in where you just went to church on Sundays in order to check that box off your list. Once again, shatter the box. You have the opportunity to walk in the authority God has given His children. Dive into His presence. Be intentional about spending time in His presence. It is your responsibility to train up a generation of world-changers, and you can't teach them how to press into the presence of God if you aren't doing it yourself. We have a higher calling and it is so much bigger than any of us. God is moving and God is speaking; let's press into Him. Let's equip ourselves in order to equip the children we are called to.

Chapter 7

Those Dreaded Words

Equipping ourselves is something that I feel like adults don't do nearly enough. I don't know if it is because we are so busy or just lack of priority, but making time to invest in yourself is one of the most precious gifts you can give those around you. As educators, we expect our students to learn and to ask questions when they don't know the correct answer. We need to do the same. Be a life-long learner, not just because it sounds good but because it is truly good for you. This way of thinking will be vital to you reaching your full potential.

Okay, I am going to say the dreaded words … professional development. Come on, don't roll your eyes. I know, I know, those words, especially coming from a principal, are dreaded. Why has professional development become something so many dread? This makes me sad because it doesn't have to be that way.

If you are an administrator reading this, I am begging you to spend the money on quality professional development—*it is worth it!* If you don't have a budget for this, make professional development time a time that your team enjoys. This should be a time of refreshing and refueling, a time to build and strengthen relationships on your team. I am not talking about cheesy games (although if your team needs to loosen up a little, maybe they need cheesy games). I am talking about really getting to know your team and being in tune with their needs. If everything you plan to do at your meeting can be addressed in an email, you are doing it so wrong. You're going to get sick of me saying this (if you aren't already), but shatter the box! Create moments during this time together that are memorable. Reward them for working so hard. They pour their heart and soul into the students in their classrooms every single day, and appreciation and letting them know that you see them and you see what they bring to the table goes such a long way. This doesn't have to cost money, although if you have the budget, please shower them with love. This can simply be you taking time out of your meeting to tell them that you see them. Encouragement makes such a difference.

At LCA, we have a staff development day once a month. It lasts three hours, and the academy is a very busy, very over-the-top place, so we almost always have a lot of content to cover. Some months we have so much to discuss that we spend the majority of the time planning and going over upcoming events. No matter what is going on, I make it a priority to set aside time to share my heart, pray, and worship together. Our monthly meetings are some of our most precious times together. Our team jokingly says that all we do is "pray and cry" at our meetings, and we love it that way. Please never forget that most educators out there do not have the opportunity or the freedom of "praying and crying" at a professional development meeting, but we do! Don't waste this gift we have. There is power in prayer, and when we pray together, we are strengthened in a supernatural way. Administrators, please find a way to pour into them; please make sure that they have time together to refuel. Let your team have time to talk about things going on in their lives outside of school. Let them laugh with each other. Embrace the times when it takes you a minute to get everyone's attention because they are talking with each other and laughter is exploding from the room. This is fuel. This is community. *This time is needed!* Time together filled with laughter is good for the soul.

This will strengthen your team unlike any team-building activity.

Teachers, take time to equip yourself. This has to be a priority. Run your race and stay focused on watering your classroom "grass," but also look and see what other educators are doing. There are some dynamic educators out there completely revolutionizing education. Research them. Use resources; that is what they are there for. Creativity is everywhere. Slow down and take it all in. Go to museums. Read books. Take time to learn. Never stop learning. Never get to a place where you think you are beyond learning.

Learn from your students, and when you are wrong or make a mistake, apologize to them. Learn from the teacher across the hall or the teacher in the other building; that's right, walk over there and ask questions. Every now and then, use your planning period to observe a co-worker just because you admire them and want to learn from them.

Harry S. Truman once said, "It's amazing what you can accomplish if you do not care who gets the credit." Listen to a podcast. Sit in your classroom and think without any distractions. Some of my best ideas as a teacher have come from getting quiet and sitting in thought. Deep thought is rare and if you can force yourself to do it, and amazing things will come from that time. Make time for learning; I can't stress this enough. This has to be an intentional habit. It is not something that will just happen. Life is busy and it will never slow down long enough; you have to set aside time for it. Make the decision that you are worth it, and just do it. Even if no one around you is growing, make the choice to grow anyway. Decide to believe that you are worth the investment, because it is true. If you don't have admin or anyone spending the time and money to equip you, equip yourself.

No one will ever care about you the way you care about you. That is just the cold, hard truth. If you don't make it happen, you will let years go by living a mediocre life as a mediocre teacher when you could have been thriving in so many areas. Don't settle for that! We tell our students to never stop learning; we need to do the same. Don't let pride get in the way of you being the best version of yourself. Dig in. Find resources. Ask for help from someone doing it well, no matter what "it" is. Find a way to make it happen. There are far too many tools and resources out there to go around thinking we know it all. Don't be that person. Equip yourself with the tools you need to be successful and commit yourself to a life where you never stop learning.

Make a commitment to yourself to bring excitement and energy into your classroom every single day.

One of my favorite things our team does happens each summer. We have a three-day staff development that is teacher-led. I began to think that I could stand up and tell my team how to do things, but really, our team was thriving. Not perfect, because we can always get better, but we were thriving. We had a 98 percent re-enrollment rate with 32 percent growth in students registered, having to turn down 72 kids because we were out of physical space, and 100 percent of our team was returning. It really couldn't get much better than the position we were in. With these thoughts running through my head, I made the decision to flip the script. Remember, if the plan doesn't work, change the plan—but never the goal. The goal was to have three days of team building, quality time in worship and prayer, and to grow individually in areas where we needed to improve. Keeping this goal in mind, I wrote down each team member on a sheet of paper. Next to their name, I wrote down one thing that I thought they were exceptional at. I soon realized that everyone had different exceptionalities. From this list, I structured our three-day staff development. I then called my team and told them my plan. I went on to tell them what I thought they should share because of their unique gift in that area. The response was amazing. When you have tools and you are given the opportunity to share what you know and what you do well, and then in return others share the things they know and do well, people grow. This doesn't mean that the teachers on our team who prefer talking to kids and not adults didn't have moments of pure hatred toward me for forcing them to get out of their comfort zone, but once they did it, they all agreed that it was so beneficial. As educators, we know it to be true that when a student has to teach a concept, we really see if they understand it or not. One of the best ways to see if a student has learned a concept is to have them teach it. It's the same in our adult lives. If you have figured something out, share it with someone else.

So why don't we do this more? Why does society tell us to withhold information? Why do we feel we need to?

Chapter 8

Withholding Information

My sister gave me a tool that completely changed the game of cooking for me. It was a tip that was very simple, and it happened in a casual group text. She told me to use rotisserie chicken in almost any dish I was making that required chicken. Y'all, for real, if you don't do this, start now! You see, I am not a great cook. I am not terrible, but I am far from good. This was a trick that truly changed the game for me when it came to cooking. It was a simple trick, but it opened up so many new meal ideas for me. Her taking a moment out of her day to share this with me opened up so many doors and saved me so much time.

This was such a silly thing, but it changed so much for me. We all have "tools" that we have learned that make life easier or better. Some things we share with others and other things we choose to withhold. I don't know if it makes us feel like we are better than others to have a skill that we have acquired and then keep it to ourselves. We have developed this mindset of "It's a dog eat dog world out there," and in some cases and environments that is true, but there are so many situations where we can truly be better together.

In the environment I am responsible for, I have over forty team members. Ninety-eight percent of them are women. I am not necessarily saying women are worse at this, but I am a woman, so I am drawing from my own experiences. One of the things I have worked so hard to create is an environment where we are all team players. I have been a part of many environments where competition was the way things were done. Having an environment full of women who operate *together* is not something that simply happens. It takes everyone working together to maintain unity. We all know that we are only as strong as our weakest link, and no one wants to be that link.

Have you ever seen someone doing something in the field you are in and it made you nauseated at how far ahead of you (or better than you) they were? Almost to the point that you didn't want to even see what they were doing because of the insecurities that would rise up in you? Maybe not. Maybe it's just me, but I have a hard time believing that is true. I went through years of feeling this way. Not just with people in education, though. I would see other women who seemed to have it all together. They planned perfect parties, dressed so cute, were in shape, had the "perfect" lives. I was trapped in the comparison game. Social media played a role in this, sure, but it wasn't just social media. I would try to look like or sound like other women only to fall short again and again. I think, whether we admit it or not, we all have this insecurity inside of us in some area of our lives.

I lived with this insecurity for years. But somewhere along the way, something shifted. I didn't realize it right away, but I know exactly when the shift began.

I met someone who began that shift in my life. Have you ever just met someone, and from the moment you met them you just hit it off as if you had known them your whole life? Well, Kelli was this person for me. We met in 2013, and just like that, we were the best of friends. We have so much in common. We soon discovered that we married our husbands on the exact same day, at the exact same time, and had the exact same colors in our wedding. It has almost become comical how much we have in common. I met her when she enrolled her daughter in my school. Her mom was actually my kindergarten teacher, and I had just hired her mom to teach our third and fourth grade class (back in the day, our grade levels were combined). After a year of getting to know Kelli, she asked me to meet her and her husband for lunch. I'll never forget that lunch. At the time, she lived about an hour away from us. We are from small towns, so an hour each way is a *long* way to drive for school where I live. She approached me with an idea of starting a school just like LCA where she lives. She certainly didn't need my blessing to do so, but she told me something that stuck with me when I told her to go for it. She told me that partnering with me to create an environment like the one we had at LCA was essential. This was a precious moment for me. I knew that what we had at LCA was amazing, but hearing that someone saw what I saw and wanted to recreate it in their town was such a special moment for me. Something happened in me that day. I knew what I was doing had value, but someone I loved and respected saw it, too. She not only saw it, she wanted me to help her recreate it. She wanted to dedicate her life to building something amazing based on something that I had built.

I was honored. I knew that I had something to offer. I also remembered starting out and wishing that someone out there would give me the tools (any tools) to make it happen.

And so our partnership began. Through the years, our schools have grown and so has our friendship. Every tool I have, I have done my best to give to her and her team, and every time we have a conversation, we are both better because of it. I have learned so much from her. What started as me teaching her has turned into a beautiful partnership between two people living similar lives. This is what happens when we equip others. It's not just for them; oftentimes it is for us as well. If we can get past feeling the need to withhold information for fear that someone will be "better than us," something really amazing happens:

We all get better, and lives are changed!

I don't want to go through life with tools and insight into situations that could possibly help someone and then just keep it to myself. It is human nature for us to keep ideas to ourselves. I would like to challenge the status quo. I have seen first-hand the benefits of mentoring others who are attempting things I have already been through. They are able to skip some of the hard stuff and it helps them. But I have also seen the way mentorship benefits the mentor. Through giving insight and inspiring others to do what you know how to do, a confidence grows within you. After seeing the benefits of mentoring, I have since helped other principals going through hard situations, and I have grown in my confidence within my own team. The more tools I have given away, the more God has given me. The principle of giving applies in every area, and this is no exception.

I am no longer the insecure girl I once was. I know who I am and I know who I am not.

I know I don't like throwing elaborate Pinterest-worthy birthday parties … so I don't.

I know I don't enjoy meal prep … so I don't.

I know I enjoy traveling … so I do!

I know I hate shopping … so my husband (who loves shopping) does all the Christmas, grocery, and birthday shopping.

I no longer let the things that society says "moms should do" make me feel insecure and less than.

I know I have insight to offer. I know I do certain things really well. I know I am incredible in certain areas. I know that I am terrible in others. I *choose* to focus on the things I am good at, and then … I share with those around me all the tricks I have found to doing those things well.

We all have "tools" in our toolbelt. We gain these "tools" by going through situations and, more likely than not, we figure out how not to do something before learning how to do it. We go through our childhood gaining tools every single day. We start the day not knowing how to do something and end the day knowing how to do it. Educators give away tools to their students on a daily basis. It's very common for people to think of teachers as individuals who give away insight and knowledge. But what happens when we get older? We know how to give away insight, because we have seen it modeled for at least thirteen years in grade school, but something happens when we get older. All of a sudden, we feel this "survival of the fittest" mindset kicking in. Something starts to shift in the way we think, and so when we gain insight, we feel the need to keep it to ourselves, to be the best. Be the best version of you. Never stop growing. Then pull someone else up with you.

I am competitive by nature. If you are an Enneagram fan, I am a 3. My natural tendency is to want to be the best. I know that about myself and I own it. There is absolutely nothing wrong with wanting to be the best. The problem is when you want others to fail, when you want to blow other candles out so that yours shines brighter. Strive to be the best. Please do! Strive to be the best version of yourself. Strive to have the best school. Strive to be the best teacher. Strive to constantly improve, but also take the time to build up those around you. One thing I have truly learned with time is a Biblical principle that when you give, it will be given unto you—pressed down, shaken together, and running over! It is true. It is the Word of God and it cannot lie!

When we allow others to equip us with tools that make us better, we are also equipping them. For so many years, I let my weaknesses be something that I tried to hide. I wanted to be good at everything, but because I wasn't, I felt the need to hide the areas I wasn't as strong in. Over time, I have learned to embrace the areas where I am not strong. I have learned to bring people into my life who are strong where I am weak. I surround myself with people who are exceptional at things that I suck at! This comes into play in building a strong culture within an organization, but it is also helpful in life. The moment we put our pride aside and embrace the fact that we can learn something from everyone we meet, then we will really begin to grow into the best version of ourselves.

If you struggle with receiving insight and new ways of thinking from those around you, I challenge you to pray that God will help you in this area. Pray that you can lay your pride aside and really hear what the people around you who you see are doing things well have to say. He will show up, and when you open yourself up to learning new ways of doing things, you will shatter the box that you have lived in for so long. There is a great big world out there full of resources and tools. Don't let pride keep you trapped in a box, thinking that is the only way to live.

Don't hoard information. Don't hoard resources. Give. Share. Equip others who need what you know, and trust that when you do, He will show up and stay true to His Word. The principle of giving is true. Test it out if you don't believe me. You want to grow in knowledge and resources? Give away knowledge and resources. What is something that you can think of right now, as you are reading this, that you do really well? What is something that someone has complimented you on when it comes to your teaching style? Has another teacher commented on the way you do something well and you knew that you could give her pointers that took you years to learn? I want to challenge you to tell her what you did. Perhaps you have incredible classroom management and that new teacher across the hall is having a very hard time keeping her students focused. Maybe you sit at lunch with your junior high kids and spend the first month of the school year focused on getting to know their hobbies. Maybe you know that developing trust and understanding helps in your classroom because there is mutual respect between you and your students. Perhaps you hear the kids talking about how "mean" that teacher is and you worry that if you give her those pointers they will then like her more than you, and you prefer being the teacher whom the kids like. Sounds petty? When it's written out like that it does, but we all know that thoughts like this want to creep in. Maybe not this exact scenario, but we all have allowed pride to creep in and cause us to not be the version of ourselves that we are proud of. We have all done things that cause us to not be the best version of ourselves; maybe it's out of fear, maybe it's out of pride, but we have all made choices similar to this. It doesn't make sense to give and to trust that new ideas will come to us; I know that, but it is true and it works, nonetheless. Let's become better by equipping others with the tools to do what we know we do well.

As educators in Christian schools, we have to rise up in every area. If you are not challenging your students with more rigorous content than any other school in your district, you are doing those kids an injustice. As Christians, we are called to a life of excellence. *Do not* water it down. If you truly want to raise up world-changers, you had better be equipping them with every single tool out there. If they leave your school and truly feel called to the medical field but aren't prepared academically to earn that degree, you haven't done your job in raising up that world-changer. Wow! That's harsh, I know, but it is the absolute truth. If you have a tool in your toolbelt that could equip a child to reach his or her full potential, why would you withhold it? If they decide they want to create the next Bible app or start the next online ministry but you haven't exposed them to the technology to learn, you haven't done your job. I know that is harsh, but we are called to show others the God way of doing things. As Christians, we are representations of Christ on the earth. Let's give it everything we have! Let's raise the standard of education. Let's be a part of the change we so desperately need to see in education. Will it require more work? Absolutely. What is this dream going to cost you? Everything. We have to realize that it's not about us. It's not about our comfort and our Monday-to-Friday schedule. It's not about having the same schedule as your kids. Let's rise up! It is time to show the world around us the heart of God. Let's teach outside of the book. Let's not just teach outside of the box, let's shatter it.

Get them up, get them moving. Every single day, something out of the ordinary should happen in your classroom. Yes, that's right, I said every day. How much more receptive to information are you when you are somewhere you want to be? Chances are, that answer is a lot. Your students are the same. Make it an exciting place to be. It doesn't have to cost money to do this. Take them outside, let them do their work under their desk, make it a silly-sock day. Some days it may be a complete room transformation, but other days you may just do language first thing when you normally do math. It may be that you added music —I suggest doing this daily; music sets the environment in such a great way. Just do what it takes to keep them engaged.

Instructing your students to open a book, read the chapter, and answer questions should never be something that comes out of your mouth. Create experiences. Make it fun. *You can do it!* I know you can! You will be able to equip them so much better if they are excited to be in your classroom. Think outside of the box! You are capable of so much more than you realize. Commit to doing it. You will be amazed at how well you can equip them when you have created an environment that they are excited to be in.

Chapter 9

Wait! Am I Smart?

I'll never forget the day I was sitting in a psychology class at LSU. The professor would ask a question and then call a name to answer it. They were practical questions on childhood development, and in a class of around one hundred students, the answers people were giving didn't make sense to me. I knew they were incorrect answers, and I was shocked that so many people didn't know the correct response. My wheels started turning and I know I was staring at my classmates in utter confusion.

You see, I grew up in a small town in Louisiana—population 4,000. I graduated with sixty-eight people. I had gone to pre-K through twelfth grade with that same small group of people. I knew and loved those classmates well. Growing up, I never thought of myself as "smart." Never.

I was always in trouble in school. I was very outgoing and always had lots of friends, but I just never thought I was very smart. I failed Algebra 1 in high school and had to retake it my sophomore year. After that, I maintained Cs throughout my high school years. It's not that I applied myself and couldn't make the grades; I just didn't think I was that smart, so I never really tried.

I left that small town to attend LSU, which had a population on campus of 30,000. So, to my surprise, when I was sitting in this psychology class, I was very confused by the fact that no one in the class knew the correct answers. I left class that day and went out to the lakes on campus. I sat with my back against a giant oak tree and stared at the water. It was a day I will never forget. Something came over me and, all of a sudden, I started to question my intelligence.

Was I actually intelligent? Had I been wrong all along? Maybe it was a fluke. I was so confused.

I wasn't sure, but I was determined to find out. I started sitting front and center in all of my classes (I had sat at the back my entire life because that was where the average but cool kids sat, and that was how I had always labeled myself.) I started engaging in lessons. I interacted with the professors. I started making straight As. I couldn't explain it, but a mindset change happened in me that day.

Something I never knew to be true was discovered that day. I had what it took to be incredibly successful, and I was determined to do it. Every dream I had, I was going to achieve it. Every goal I set: done!

There is a quote by Steve Jobs that says,

"The moment you realize that everything in the world around you was built by people who were no smarter than you, you become an element of change yourself … you can change anything."

This became so true in my life—this idea of not only finding something that needed to change but being the change I wanted to see in the world and truly embracing the idea that I could actually do it. This was life-changing for me. I began to dive into research on education. I learned about what was working and what wasn't. For me, education was the thing I wanted to change; it was the thing that had made me feel "less than" in my own life. It took me until the age of nineteen to realize that I wasn't dumb, and it didn't happen overnight. That was where the process of breaking the cycle began for me. I wanted to take and shatter all the things that were being done incorrectly and making kids feel anything but empowered. I was on a mission, but before I could venture out and change education, I had to change my own mindset about who I was.

You see, I knew all the motivational scriptures. I am fearfully and wonderfully made. I am created in His image. I am above and not beneath. The list goes on and on, but I never believed those things. I never felt worthy. I never felt like I had much to offer the world. For me, it wasn't an overnight thing. The process of breaking this mindset away from my life was a slow one. But it was a necessary process of preparation.

When you are growing up, there are people who say hurtful things to you, but it's nothing like when you grow up and start to see a glimpse of success. If you are doing something, *anything*, with your life, people will have an opinion about it. Those opinions will hurt, and they are more than likely to come from those closest to you—at least in the beginning. You will not be able to overcome and be successful without a season of empowering yourself to face the challenges life throws at you. Nothing can truly prepare you for the pain you will face in life, but knowing who you are and being confident in that sure does help. I have had seasons where my character was questioned, my integrity was run through the trash, and my motives were lied about. I am far from perfect, and I have made massive mistakes. But I know who I am. I know my strengths and I know my shortcomings. I know what motivates me and I know what I am just not going to do, no matter how much someone thinks I should.

I am so tired of seeing people who have taken the negative words spoken over them and have ultimately allowed those negative words to tell them who they are and who they aren't. Why would we allow others to dictate who we are and who we are not? There is only *one person* with that authority: *our creator*, and He says that we are fearfully and wonderfully made. He says we are the head and not the tail. He says we are more than conquerors.

It is time to step it up; we (the children of God) have to *rise up*. We have to realize that when we discredit or bash the product (ourselves or others) that we are ultimately discrediting or bashing the manufacturer (God). We would never say, "God sucks at making things, and the things He makes are worthless." But when we speak death over ourselves *or* over others, that is *exactly* what we are saying.

Let's make a choice to be a light in the darkness. Let's choose to wake up each day and tell ourselves how amazing we are, and then go out and speak life over those whom we encounter on a daily basis. It doesn't take much to make someone's day better; it simply takes us slowing down long enough to notice the good in others. Make a plan and stick to it.

But how?

It's easy for me to sit here on the other side and give you my opinion on what you should or shouldn't do. In fact, we have become a people that do just that far too often. Anyone and everyone who has access to social media is a critic and has an opinion about the lives of others. Opinions are at an all-time high.

Here is the reality: You are going to mess up. You are going to fall flat on your face. You will try something and it won't work the way you wanted it to. One thing I have learned in the past decade of leading an organization is that you have to make decisions and just go with them. Allow yourself to make a decision even without all the answers. Gather as much information as you can, but trust yourself and trust that if you are seeking God, He will guide you every step of the way. Do it or don't. Buy it or don't. It honestly doesn't matter what "it" is; make a decision. There is serious risk in hesitation. Have you ever seen something that was invented that you thought about years before it came out and you thought to yourself, "I should've invented that when I thought of it"? *Everyone* has ideas. Everyone thinks of solutions to problems. They may not know how to make it, but they know what is needed to resolve certain problems. The issue is not a lack of ideas;

the thing that stops people from actually accomplishing something is that they aren't willing to do what it takes to get there. They aren't willing to empower themselves in order to face the obstacles that will come when you do something that involves risk. Are you willing to risk what it will cost to do what you want to do? It doesn't matter if it's something you want to do in your classroom or if it's an idea you want to bring into the world. It's going to cost you. You want to start a different teaching technique? Are you willing to be criticized? You want to do a room transformation? Are you willing to put in the hours or days that will take? You want to create something that will change education for the better? What are you willing to try to bring it to pass? You have to empower yourself and you have to jump. Jump off the cliff and build your wings on the way down. Maybe that sounds super dangerous, but in my experience, hesitation is more dangerous. Hesitation leads to overthinking and eventually talking yourself out of it.

You have to learn how to give yourself grace. *You are going to mess up!* You are going to miss the mark, and you are going to fall short over and over again. Don't keep reliving it. If it's sin, ask for forgiveness and *move on!* Life is too short to live in a defeated state of mind. God's Word says He casts our sin as far as the east is from the west. He is over it, so you should be too! If in the process of your sin you hurt someone (as we often do), ask for their forgiveness, and if you don't receive it, *move on*! Once again, life is just too short!

We empower ourselves in so many ways, but I would dare to say that the best thing we can do is to allow ourselves to fail. We grow by overcoming failure. Give yourself grace and strive to see yourself the way Christ sees you. He has such amazing things to say about His children. He loves us so much and gives grace so freely. We have to give this same grace to ourselves and learn from our mistakes, overcome, and move on! When we do this, we empower ourselves to try again. Life is a series of trying and falling short, but we just have to keep getting back up and trying again. Trust that it is part of the process. Trust that God works all things together for the good of those who love Him and are called according to His purpose. You don't know what is on the other side of the pain. I have seen God's hand over and over again in situations that I didn't think could possibly turn around. I don't believe God causes the pain, but I do believe He will use it. I believe that sometimes it is necessary in order to bring His plan to fruition. His ways are higher than our ways and His thoughts are higher than our thoughts.

There is a tree called the lodgepole pine. A lodgepole pine is a highly adaptable tree that can grow in all sorts of environments. They can grow in bogs or sand. It's also one of the first trees to grow after a forest fire. They have something called serotinous cones that are sealed with resin. They actually require fire to grow. The heat of a fire melts the resin, which allows it to open. When it opens, it begins the growing process and becomes a beautiful tree filled with almost elastic-like branches that are very difficult to break. This is such a perfect example of what it takes to be successful and thrive in whatever area is being pursued. We have to be willing to be put under fire in order to remove the things that are keeping us bound and closed off to growth. Is the fire fun? Absolutely not. Is the fire necessary? Absolutely.

What comes from the ashes is beautiful. What rises from destruction is a stronger, more empowered person. Don't give up because it's getting hot. Don't quit when you see the smoke in the distance heading your way. Face it full on, knowing that God is with you and He is for you. If God is for you, then who can be against you? Trust the process, and fight with everything in you to rise from the ashes when the smoke settles, knowing that you will be stronger and better than ever. You can stand with the knowledge that you are incredible. You are royalty. You are a child of the most high God, and He is with you. Empower yourself with that knowledge. Feel empowered with the understanding that if you're still breathing, then He is not finished. Don't give up and don't give in. He brings beauty from ashes.

Chapter 10

Empowering Others

For years, my phone didn't stop. It would ring from morning to night. If a student had a dentist appointment the following day, I would get a text about it at 9 p.m. the night before. For years this was my norm, and I truly didn't mind. I liked the feeling of being needed. I didn't care in what capacity; I just wanted to be the one who was needed. This led to me being the principal who would intercept parents before they could talk to their teacher because I thought I could handle it better.

By nature, I like to be in control of situations. I do not have trouble making decisions, and I am not one of those types of people who says, "I don't care" when asked where we should eat. I know what I want, and I don't have trouble pushing through whatever obstacle is in front of me to get it. I am, however, very particular about how I like things done. This bleeds into a lot of areas of my life, but when it comes to my organization, I am *very* particular. When we first started, I wanted to just do it all myself because the fear of how someone else would do anything would scare me. I am not exaggerating when I say that the school had been established for *years* before I purchased a school phone. I hired a front office manager and had no phone for her because I used my cell phone. She purchased a phone and it still took a solid year for me to use it. This is not a joke! If you were to ask my team today if I empower them to make their own decisions within their classroom, they would definitely say that I do. In fact, I did an anonymous survey asking them if that was true before I wrote what they would say. One hundred percent of my team said that I empower them to do their thing! So how did this change take place? To start with, I came to an understanding when I heard a quote by Craig Groeschel, "You can have control, or you can have growth, but you can't have both." This quote can certainly apply to business, which was its original intent, but it also applies to our daily lives as well as our classrooms.

Are you empowering your students? Do you give them a task and leave room for them to do it in a way that gets a great result but that may look different from the way you would have done it?

Empowering our students looks different depending on their age, but the principle still applies. In private or Christian schools, we have parents who have a certain expectation, so it is very easy for us to just do it for them or spoon-feed them in order to get a good grade on their report card. Parents are happy with the (unearned) A, the admin is happy because no parents are upset, and you are happy because you kept the peace. I get it. Believe me, I do. We are in a tricky business because it is a business, but it's also a ministry, but then it's a school. How in the world do we balance those three things? Sadly, what I see more than I care to mention in private or Christian schools is a mentality of just keep the peace, keep everyone happy, and keep enrollment up.

But what about the child? What about the product that we are on a mission to raise or to produce, for lack of a better word? How is just keeping the peace going to create a mighty warrior fully equipped for the challenges and adversity ahead? How does keeping the peace raise a world-changer? There is one simple answer: It doesn't. I know this isn't what you want to hear, but I am here to shatter the box of the way things have always been done. If collecting the tuition check and keeping the peace is your mission, by all means, carry on. I am talking to those of you who truly believe in your students, those of you who have given your lives for this. If you truly see potential in those kids, challenge them, encourage them, equip them, and empower them. Tell them you believe in them and then actually believe in them!

I am not saying that you need to ruffle feathers and go against the authority in place. I am saying: challenge your students because you truly believe in them. I promise you, when parents see the product that this produces, they will begin to truly trust the process. Explain to them that you push because you believe in them, that you see so much potential in them, because you do!

Parents ultimately want what is best for their child. It is our job as the educator to communicate with parents and keep them in the loop. When they see your heart and trust that you have the very best intentions for their child, they will be much more open to the challenge ahead.

In addition to challenging your students, *please* empower your teammates! Back them up and support them at all costs. If they make mistakes, encourage them and say that they will get it right the next time. Please don't throw them under the bus. Have each other's back. You all know how hard this job is, so support each other and build each other up.

Empowering others simply means trusting them first and giving them grace when they mess up. Just like we discussed earlier in this book, people mess up. People will fail you, and when you truly empower people around you, you are guaranteed to be disappointed. So why the heck would you want to empower others? Truthfully, it goes back to that quote, because we want to grow, and we want those around us to grow and be the best they can be.

When COVID-19 hit the United States, mass chaos broke out. If you were an educator during this time, I want to say *great job*! Educators from all over the United States stepped up to the challenge of educating children through technology and other resources in a way that had never been seen before.

It was a Friday morning at 5:45 when I looked online and saw that Ohio, Michigan, and Maryland had closed schools. I immediately knew that this decision was coming our way. I sat quietly in my living room and prayed for direction. I knew that we needed to be prepared and we needed to act fast. I wanted to have our next steps in place and get ahead of the news in the best way I could. When I felt like I had a general idea of what we would do, I sent a video message to my team letting them know that a shutdown was more than likely headed our way and that we needed to be proactive. We decided to spend that day working on laying out details of the plan and getting ahead of it. When the decision was announced at 1:30 that afternoon, we immediately sent a message informing parents of what we had in mind. We had been preparing all day, so to us this had been a long-thought-out process, but our families were blown away at our rapid response. Our team quickly went into get-it-done mode. We decided to continue their education via online learning. We got packets of work together all weekend and had them ready for pickup that Sunday at 2 p.m. Videos of their teachers giving instructions and teaching lessons were sent out each night via email. It was as flawless as it could possibly be. However, it was *a lot* of work that my team was given during a very stressful situation. They were immediately expected to work through the weekend to get content ready with no notice. The videos were unbelievable, and they not only pulled it off, but they absolutely killed it! I was so proud and blown away by them.

They all had moments in the middle of it when they thought that they couldn't pull it off, but they pushed through. When all the work was done, one of my team members sent me a text that spoke volumes to me. She said, "You empowered a group of women who stress out about talking on a microphone at our awards programs to video themselves teaching and share it on a public platform. What I know is true about this situation is that it wasn't really anything you said throughout this stressful situation (though your words were helpful, obviously). What I believe really did it were the hundred staff meetings where you said that it isn't about us, it's bigger, and that we are awesome, and that we are capable, and that God has called us to something huge. It was the trust that has been built up for years, so in the moment of crisis, when you tell us all those things, we believe you because you've been saying them forever." This text was the epitome of empowering others, in my opinion. You can't just tell someone one time that you believe in them and expect them to do it. You have to give opportunities over and over again, and when they fail, don't freak out. Just give them words of reassurance and help them come up with a solution for getting back up.

Empowering others is developed over time, but if you truly want to see the best in someone, let them try. Let them do it even if it isn't the way you would do it. Let them know when they mess up that it's okay, that we all do. Whether it is your student or another team member, we have to empower those around us. Let's be that safe place for people to spread their wings and try to fly. If you do this enough, something beautiful will come from it.

If you are an administrator, please let your team try new things! If it ends up being a terrible idea, they will figure that out! But what if it works? What if it's an idea that makes the school better? What if it's exactly what you needed? Each person on your team is full of ideas that they need to be given the freedom to voice. Be that safe place for them. Trust me, they see problems that you do not see! You need them to feel comfortable going to you. I don't care how great your team is, you have problems or you have potential problems that could be resolved if those in the trenches were free to voice their concerns and knew that they would truly be heard.

Chapter 11

Their Voice Matters

Have you ever felt like nothing you say matters? I think we have all had situations or relationships where we felt like it really didn't matter what we said, it wasn't going to make a difference. Maybe you just aren't someone's cup of tea and you know it. The feeling of someone not caring about what you have to say is tough. No one wants to have these emotions.

On the other hand, have you ever been in a relationship or had a conversation with someone who was very interested in what you had to say? It's incredible when you truly experience being valued and like your voice and the words you speak truly matter.

As an educator, we have a responsibility to be intentional about empowering our students. We have to take time to give them a voice and let them know that their voice matters! We have to make sure they know that they bring value to this world. If we are truly going to raise up an army of world-changers, we have to make sure they know that their voice matters and their voice creates change. This starts at a very early age. One way that we have learned to practice this is that when students show up at school, we say, "Good morning!" and they are required to speak back. This seems like such a simple thing, but even as young as three years old they naturally want to walk past without speaking because they are tired or just distracted. We teach them to slow down, make eye contact, and speak.

We also encourage parents to allow their child to order their own food in a restaurant and ask for a refill when they need it. Little, everyday things like this get them to understand that their voice matters and their voice creates change. It doesn't take a huge speaking opportunity. This is taught over time. This is a skill that is developed through repetition.

I'll never forget the day a group of eighth graders came up to me and told me that they felt like it was an "injustice" that they had to walk in a line from one building to another. They weren't saying this in a disrespectful way; they just had very strong feelings about it. The reason that this policy was in place was because we are a pre-K through eighth grade school, so we know they have little eyes on them, and we want them to set a good example. I simply told them to schedule an appointment and we would sit down and talk through their "grievances."

When a student comes up to you with a genuine concern, I want to challenge you to be sure not to discredit their passion, even if you feel like it is something silly. To them it is a big deal or they wouldn't be coming to you, so use it as an opportunity for them to have their voice heard.

These students scheduled a meeting as instructed. It was scheduled for the following day during their recess time. I arranged for their teachers, our academic director, and myself to be there. They entered the meeting well dressed and shook our hands before sitting down. We sat in my office and heard them out. We went through the things that they felt needed to change, and we agreed to most of them in exchange for a few things I was wanting from them—more participation and leadership responsibilities. We ended the meeting and we were all very happy with how it went. They had a concern, they came to the person who had authority to make a change (in this case it was me), and they saw change occur. Y'all, this is a powerful lesson! This isn't something that just happens. This is years of them coming to me or their teachers and having that adult stop what they are doing, look them in the eye, and hear them. This is how you raise up world-changers: one thoughtful conversation at a time. They have to know they are valuable and that they matter.

Do we always get it right? No.

Are there days when we get busy and rush through without slowing down? Absolutely.

But more often than not, we stop and listen. They know their voice creates change, and this is a very, very powerful lesson.

What is the goal? To raise up a world-changer. In order to do this, they need to not only be prepared academically and spiritually, but they need to be able to introduce themselves and speak up when they see an injustice. When you keep the end goal in mind, you will start to see teachable moments in everyday situations. Start to look for them if you aren't already doing so. If you feel busy and overwhelmed, force yourself to slow down and listen anyway. There is so much power in this principle.

One of our kids left to head off to the great big world of high school. She entered the 5A high school and very quickly realized that they didn't have a writing club. She wanted to do something about it. She took the time to research the handbook to see how to go about starting a club. One of the requirements was that she would need a teacher sponsor. She arranged for that with her English teacher; then she was ready. She scheduled a meeting with the school principal, entered the office, shook her hand, and introduced herself. She informed her that she was a 4.0 student with a passion for writing and that she had noticed that the school was lacking a writing club. She went on to explain that she had arranged for a teacher sponsor prior to meeting with her. The principal was very impressed and immediately gave her a yes! These are just a few stories of what empowerment does. Raising up world-changers doesn't just happen, and it won't just happen without having people who are intentional and speaking life into them. It also won't just happen without people who let them try something and fail. When they realize that there really aren't very many situations that you can't bounce back from, they will start to be less fearful of taking that leap. This is our job as educators. This is what we have to do for our students. We have to empower. It truly doesn't matter how old they are, there are opportunities to give them a voice.

I challenge you to dig deep for ways to make your students feel seen and heard. Slow down and truly listen to them. Look them in the eye and listen to what they have to say. When they realize that their voice matters and their voice creates change, there is absolutely no limit to what they can accomplish!

Chapter 12

Teach Them to Seek Him

Each year, we take our eighth graders away for three days. We take them to a campground and completely disconnect. We make it our mission to not take very many pictures—we will usually only take one on the day they arrive. We want them to have an opportunity to connect with God in a raw and real way. We have breakout sessions and, to be honest with you, the gloves come off. We are giving them all the tools left in our toolbelt before they head off to high school. During this time that we set aside for growth in Christ, something beautiful happens. We give them tools for pressing in and seeking God, and then we give them opportunities to do so. Every year, God shows up in a powerful way. We explain to them that life is hard, things don't always go the way we want them to, and disappointment happens. We tell them that at the end of the day, it's not our relationship with God that will help them; it's not their parents' relationship with Him, either. Their life depends on them knowing God for themselves. The only thing that will get them through this life is a true relationship with Christ and then knowing how to worship Him and seek Him for themselves. We have chapel each week and they worship God during that time, but there is something so raw about getting away from the distractions of the world and not only using this time for fun and team-building games (we do all of that), but really it is about a true encounter with Jesus. And He *always* shows up!

As Christian school educators, we have an incredible opportunity. We have something that no other school has: the freedom to openly talk about Jesus and spend teaching time teaching our students about the love of God. This is one area that I feel like is either a main focus—causing the academic side to lack—or it is barely touched on. Schools that were founded on the principles of Christianity have somehow lost their way through the years. They have Christian in the name but not in their character. We have to find the balance. God is in everything we do; don't get that confused with what I am saying. I am talking about meeting together with watered-down academic lessons.

We are not a Sunday school. We are a school! Academics shouldn't suffer because we want to keep our kids in a Christian bubble. We can create a safe place for our kids to learn while equipping them for what is ahead.

It is such an injustice to kids to water down the academic side of their schooling. We have to find the balance. Spend time teaching them how to seek God for themselves; this is the only thing that will sustain them. Teach them the importance of worship. Teach them how to pray the Word of God over their lives. Show them how vital a relationship with Christ is. Don't miss this opportunity. Don't water it down. What an incredible opportunity we have. Do you realize how many Christians out there teaching in a public setting would absolutely love to have the opportunity to share the love of Christ with their students? I think we take it for granted far too often. We have such a beautiful opportunity. Let's take full advantage of the freedom we have been given to have Christ in our school.

We have an obligation as Christian school educators to teach our students how to grow in their relationship with God. Let's make it our mission not to waste a single moment when we could be pouring into them, but please remember, you can't pour from an empty cup. You need Him. You need a deep relationship with Him. You need to be praying the Word of God over your life and praying it over your students. Model this for them from a place of relationship. You are so worth it! Please hear me when I tell you that you are valuable and God loves you very much! He hasn't forgotten about you. Press in to Him. Seek Him and you will find Him, then show your students how to do the same.

They may not appreciate it at the moment, but one thing I know is that when things get hard in their lives (even when they are adults), they will remember how to press in. They will remember what you taught them and they will rise up when things are hard.

There are approximately 35,000 Christian schools in the United States alone, with five million students enrolled in them. Stop and think about what it would look like if we were to truly encourage, equip, and empower ourselves and then take those tools and do the same for these five million kids. An *army* of world-changers would arise fully prepared to bring Christ to our nation and our world in a way that has never been seen before. I believe in Christian schools. I believe that it is time for us to take a stand. No more mediocre lessons. No more mediocre learning spaces. No more doing the same old, same old way of doing things. We have the God factor; we represent God in education. Let's do things with the utmost excellence.

Let's go the extra mile. Let's be over-the-top and give our students the best of the best! Why would we not want to show others how it should be done in every area of education? This isn't to show off how amazing we are or to brag about who we are and point others to ourselves.

This is to point others to Christ; He is the one who deserves all the glory.

I know we have it in us! I know that at the core of who you are, you love God and love your students. Both of them deserve our best. Let's stand together and say enough is enough. Let's stand together and encourage, equip, and empower *ourselves first*—then show up every single day and encourage, equip, and empower *our students*. Let's stand together and

SHATTER THE BOX

that has been the status quo for as long as any of us can remember. And then let's watch God show up and do the extraordinary.

Booking.

To request Stefanee Tolbert for your next professional development or a speaking engagement:

Stolbert@lcasulphur.com

Facebook: stefaneetolbert

Instagram: stefaneetolbert